THE
Afterlife
SERIES

Living in the Light of Eternity

UNDERSTANDING DEATH, DYING, & THE AFTERLIFE

Don Stewart

Living In The Light Of Eternity
Understanding Death, Dying And The Afterlife:

© 2015 By Don Stewart

Published by Educating Our World
www.educatingourworld.com
All rights reserved

English Versions Cited
The various English versions which we cite in this book apart from the King James Version, all have copyrights. They are listed as follows.

TABLE OF CONTENTS

Living In The Light Of Eternity
Understanding Death, Dying And The Afterlife
(Volume 1 Of 5)

The thought of eternity is hard for us to comprehend. Yet eternity is something we are all facing. Indeed, it is the personal future for each and every one of us. Therefore, it is crucial that we understand how to live in light of it.

In this book, we will examine how to conduct our lives with eternity in mind. How do we live a life pleasing to God with eternity in our future?

However, before we examine this topic, it is important to understand what the Bible has to say about death, dying and the afterlife.

If God created a perfect world, then why do people die? Is there life after death? Is heaven a reality? If so, then how do we get there? Are there answers to these questions? Where do we find them?

There are indeed answers to these and other ultimate questions about death, dying and what lies beyond the grave. They are found in only one place, the Bible!

Once we answer these preliminary questions from Scripture, then we will look at how we should live in the light of eternity.

For example, how do we live a life that honors God in preparation for eternity? How do we prepare for our own death? Should Christians be afraid of dying? How do we react to the death of a loved one who is a believer? How do we react to the death of a loved one who may not be a believer? Should believers be buried or cremated upon death?

OUR FIVE VOLUME SERIES ON THE AFTERLIFE

As mentioned, this is the first volume in a series of five works on the subject of the "Afterlife."

The next book deals with the in-between state, what happens to us at the moment of death. It is titled, "What Happens One Second After We Die?"

Death is not the end of our existence. Consequently, this is followed by a book on what the Bible says about the resurrection of the dead and future judgments. We title this book, "Resurrection and Judgment."

Next we will have a volume on the subject of "Heaven;" something all people are curious about. We title it, "Heaven: The Final Destination of Believers."

Finally, to complete what the Scripture says on the "Afterlife," we have a book covering the horrific subject of "Hell." The title is, "Hell: The Final Destination of Unbelievers."

The goal of this series is to educate people as to what the Bible, the only authoritative source on these matters, has to say about death, dying, heaven and hell, the end of this life and then the afterlife. In other words, they deal with our personal future.

Why Are The Subjects Of Death, Dying, And The Afterlife Worth Studying?

As we begin our investigation of the subject of the afterlife, we will start by asking an obvious question: Why should we be engaged in such a study? Of what personal benefit is there in looking at the subjects of death, dying, heaven, and hell?

Why study about our future, when we have to live right now in the present? Could not our time and energy be better spent elsewhere?

However, all of us will greatly benefit when we examine what the Bible has to say about these subjects. This is true for the following important reasons.

REASON 1: ONLY THE BIBLE GIVES ANSWERS TO THE GREAT UNKNOWN

To begin with, there is a very practical reason as to why these subjects should be studied. Death is something that we all face and the afterlife is the great unknown. Humans everywhere would love to have answers to these ultimate questions of death, dying, and then what happens next.

Studying what the Bible has to say, will give us answers to questions about *why* we die, as well as *what* takes place after we die. Moreover, since the Bible is the *only* authoritative source on these subjects, it is important for us to know what it says about the end of this life as well as the world to come.

REASON 2: IT WILL CLEAR UP MISCONCEPTIONS ABOUT WHAT HAPPENS AFTER DEATH

Many people think that death is the end of our existence. Others believe that when Christians die they go to purgatory; a halfway place between earth and heaven. Still others think that humanity can know absolutely nothing about what takes place on "the other side."

However, when we study what the Bible has to say about these subjects any confusion that we may have can be cleared up. There is no need for uncertainty, or wrong beliefs, on these topics since God has clearly spoken to us in His Word. Therefore, there is no reason whatsoever for us to have any misconceptions about death, dying, and the afterlife.

REASON 3: THE SUBJECTS OF DEATH, DYING AND THE AFTERLIFE ARE AN IMPORTANT PART OF GOD'S WORD

Furthermore, a large part of the Bible deals with the subject of death, the dying process, and then life after death. These are issues which are covered extensively in both testaments. Indeed, much of the Bible looks forward to the final state of humanity, as well as the process that brings us to the end of this life.

Since death, dying, and the afterlife are key subjects of Scripture, they deserve to be studied by all. Indeed, they should not be neglected.

We should also note that while the Bible does not answer every question we may have about these topics it does answer *all* of the important ones.

REASON 4: IT WILL INSTILL CONFIDENCE AND HOPE IN THE BELIEVER

There are other benefits. Confidence and hope for the believer will be the result of studying what Scripture has to say about the end of this life and then of life beyond the grave.

For those of us who have trusted Jesus Christ as our Savior, we can be confident that this life is not all that there is. Something else awaits us beyond the grave; everlasting life in the presence of Almighty God! Consequently, we should live our daily lives in light of that knowledge.

In fact, the Bible stresses that eternal life with the living God is something which we believers can *know* that we possess. Indeed, the Apostle John wrote the following to the Christians of his day.

> I write these things to you who believe in the name of the Son of God, so that you may know that you have eternal life (1 John 5:13 NRSV).

He emphasized that we can *know* that we have eternal life. If we have believed in Jesus Christ, then we can be assured that something wonderful awaits us when we die. Consequently, a study of the afterlife will give us confidence and hope in this life as we prepare for eternity.

REASON 5: IT WILL HELP US MAINTAIN THE PROPER PERSPECTIVE IN THIS LIFE

When we understand that this life is not all that there is, we are able to make our daily decisions, as well as decisions about life and death, in light of eternity. This can, and should, lead us to having a proper balance in this life. Indeed, we realize that the choices we now make have eternal ramifications.

Consequently, when we begin to understand this truth, then our lives will be lived from an eternal perspective. Paul wrote about this in his letter to the Romans. He said.

> Yet what we suffer now is nothing compared to the glory he will give us later (Romans 8:18 NLT).

The suffering which we experience in this life is really nothing compared to the wonderful things which God has promised to those who believe.

REASON 6: IT GIVES US MOTIVATION FOR GODLY LIVING

A correct understanding of the afterlife should motivate Christians to godly living. Indeed, it will encourage us to live a life pleasing to God in light of what is to come. John wrote to the believers.

> And all who have this eager expectation will keep themselves pure, just as he is pure (1 John 3:3 NLT).

We purify ourselves, or keep ourselves pure, because we know there is something wonderful waiting for us in the future. Therefore, we live our lives knowing this life is not the end of our existence.

Understanding these truths is indeed very practical. For example, in the Sermon on the Mount, the Lord Jesus said that we are to have our treasures stored up in heaven rather than here upon the earth. He put it this way.

> Do not lay up for yourselves treasures on earth, where moth and rust destroy and where thieves break in and steal, but lay up for yourselves treasures in heaven, where neither moth nor rust destroys and where thieves do not break in and steal. For where your treasure is, there your heart will be also (Matthew 6:19-21 ESV).

The goal should be godly living in this life in preparation for the next life. This should always be kept foremost in our minds.

REASON 7: IT WILL GIVE US GREAT COMFORT AND ENCOURAGEMENT WHEN BELIEVERS DIE

A study of the afterlife can be a comfort and encouragement for those who have lost loved ones who have believed in Jesus Christ. Indeed, the Bible makes it clear that death is not the end. Those who have died "in Christ" will someday be reunited with their loved ones who have also believed. Knowing this can be a source of great comfort.

In fact, after speaking of this hope, the Apostle Paul wrote the following to the Thessalonians.

> Therefore comfort one another with these words (1 Thessalonians 4:18 NKJV).

Great encouragement can be gained from such a study. We can be comforted with the fact that our Christian friends and loved ones are presently with Jesus and that someday we will see them again. This is really great news!

REASON 8: IT WILL GIVE BELIEVERS COMPASSION FOR THOSE WHICH ARE LOST

One of the results from a study of the subjects of death, dying and the afterlife will be a genuine compassion for the lost. Indeed, we will begin to view people as Jesus saw them, helpless and hopeless. The Bible says the following about the Lord Jesus.

> When he saw the crowds, he had compassion for them, because they were harassed and helpless, like sheep without a shepherd. Then he said to his disciples, "The harvest is plentiful, but the laborers are few; therefore ask the Lord of the harvest to send out laborers into his harvest" (Matthew 9:36-38 NRSV).

Jesus was moved with compassion for the lost. We should have the same concern for those who do not know Him.

We also find that it is God's desire that people turn away from their sins. The Lord told Ezekiel.

> Say to them, As I live, says the Lord GOD, I have no pleasure in the death of the wicked, but that the wicked turn from their ways and live; turn back, turn back from your evil ways; for why will you die, O house of Israel? (Ezekiel 33:11 NRSV)

Understanding that every human being will spend eternity either with the Lord in heaven, or without Him in hell, should give us a sense of compassion and urgency for those who do not know Jesus Christ.

REASON 9: IT WILL SERVE AS A WARNING FOR UNBELIEVERS

Studying about the afterlife can also serve as a warning for those who have not believed in Jesus. Understanding what the future holds for them can be a strong motivation for trusting Jesus Christ as their Savior.

To illustrate this truth, Jesus told a parable about a certain man who was unprepared for the future.

> And he gave an illustration: "A rich man had a fertile farm that produced fine crops. In fact, his barns were full to over-flowing. He said to himself, 'What should I do? I don't have room for all my crops.' So he said, 'I know! I'll tear down my barns and build bigger ones. Then I'll have room enough to store everything. And I'll sit back and say to myself, 'My friend, you have enough stored away for years to come. Now take it easy! Eat, drink, and be merry!' But God said to him, 'You fool! You will die this very night. Then who will get everything you worked for?' Yes, a person is a fool to store up earthly wealth but not have a rich relationship with God (Luke 12:16-21 NLT).

From this parable of Jesus, we learn that this life should be looked at as preparation for the next. Our choices here upon the earth will determine where we will spend the next life. Like the rich man that Jesus spoke about, those who do not believe in Christ need to realize that death can come at any time. Consequently, everyone needs to be prepared to meet their Maker. Indeed, it can happen when we least expect it!

REASON 10: WE WILL REALIZE THAT JUSTICE WILL EVENTUALLY BE DONE IN THE UNIVERSE

Finally, a biblical study of death, dying and the afterlife will show us that justice will ultimately prevail in the universe. We will discover that God is in control of all things. Indeed, it is His universe. There will come a time when He will "right all the wrongs."

THE LORD REMEMBERS THE DEEDS OF BELIEVERS

In fact, the Lord has kept a record of the behavior of everyone. The prophet Malachi spoke of a "book, or scroll, of remembrance" for those who believe in the Lord. He wrote.

> Then those who feared the LORD spoke with each other, and the LORD listened to what they said. In his presence, a scroll of remembrance was written to record the names of those who feared him and always thought about the honor of his name (Malachi 3:16 NLT).

This book, or scroll, has been written for the purpose of rewarding believers, not condemning them.

THE LORD REMEMBERS THE DEEDS OF UNBELIEVERS

However, the Lord also remembers the deeds of those who have not believed in Him. We read in the Book of Revelation about the ultimate destiny of those who have rejected Him.

> Then I saw a great white throne and him who was seated on it. The earth and the heavens fled from his presence, and there was no place for them. And I saw the dead, great and small, standing before the throne, and books were opened. Another book was opened, which is the book of life. The dead were judged according to what they had done as recorded in the books. The sea gave up the dead that were in it, and death and Hades gave up the dead that were in them, and each person was judged according to what they had done. Then death and Hades were thrown into the lake of fire. The

lake of fire is the second death. Anyone whose name was not
found written in the book of life was thrown into the lake of
fire (Revelation 20:11-15 NIV)

God remembers all things. Nothing escapes Him, not a single thing.

Furthermore, we are told that God will judge everyone in a fair or righteous manner which includes paying back the wrongdoer. The Bible says.

For the wrongdoer will be paid back for whatever wrong has
been done, and there is no partiality (Colossians 3:25 NRSV).

The Apostle Paul also stated this truth to a crowd of skeptics in the city
of Athens. He said.

For he has set a day when he will judge the world with justice
by the man he has appointed. He has given proof of this to
everyone by raising him from the dead (Acts 17:31 NIV)

God's justice will eventually take place when He judges the world. This
is the consistent message of Scripture.

CONCLUSION: THE SUBJECT OF THE AFTERLIFE IS OF VAST IMPORTANCE

Because of the above reasons, we discover that the study of the afterlife
is one of tremendous personal importance.

Indeed, the biblical description of death, dying, heaven and hell is
something which each of us should take the time to understand. Once
we do so, then we can properly live our lives in the light of eternity.

SUMMARY TO QUESTION 1
**WHY ARE THE SUBJECTS OF DEATH, DYING, AND THE AFTERLIFE WORTH
STUDYING?**

Some people wonder whether the subjects of the process of dying, the
inevitability of death, and of life beyond this life are really worth taking the time to study. After all, we have to live in the "here and now."

In addition, why study about something so awful to think about such as death and dying as well as what might happen after we are gone?

However, we will not really know how to live properly in this life unless we understand what the Bible has to say about the next life.

First, there is one very practical reason as to why we ought to study about the end of this life as well as what awaits us in the next world; death is inescapable. Indeed, we are all going to die and humanly speaking we have no real answers as to what happens after death. Death is the great unknown. So, how do we conduct our lives in this life knowing that death awaits us?

Fortunately, there are answers! Indeed, it is the Bible and the Bible alone which has the authoritative answers on the subjects of death and life after death. Only the Word of God provides us with accurate information about death, dying, heaven and hell. If we want to know about this topic then we must study the Bible.

In addition, misconceptions and uncertainty about the next world will be cleared up with a biblical understanding of the afterlife. However, without a study of Scripture, the afterlife will remain a mystery to us. It will remain "the great unknown."

Moreover, a large part of Scripture is devoted to these topics. If God has dedicated a substantial part of His Word to issues regarding death, dying, and the afterlife, then it must be important. What is important to God should be important to us. Therefore, we should take the time to study these subjects.

There is also the confidence factor. For the believer in Jesus Christ, confidence and hope should result from a study of the afterlife. Death and the dying process do not have to hold us in the grip of fear. We know that there is something infinitely better that awaits us after this life is over.

There is another very practical aspect in studying about the afterlife. Decisions can now be made in light of eternity. When we understand the biblical teaching on life after death, then this will affect the way we make our life-decisions. Realizing that we will be held accountable to God should result in godly living. We will conduct our lives in such a way that will please the Lord.

In addition, this study will encourage those of us who have deceased loved ones who have believed in Jesus Christ. We realize we do not have to sorrow as those who have no hope, the unbelievers. The believing dead are presently with Jesus; they are in a much better place. We will see them again when we join them! This knowledge will certainly comfort us as we live out our daily lives.

There is also the motivation for evangelism, reaching the lost. Realizing that each individual will spend eternity either with or without Christ is a strong motivating force to reach the lost with the good news about Jesus. There is a message we need to proclaim, indeed, we must proclaim!

There is also something in this study for the unbeliever. Knowing what the future holds serves as a warning for those who do not know Jesus Christ as their Savior. Judgment is coming. What we do in this life will determine how and where we spend the next life. Studying about the afterlife makes clear the need for each individual to receive Christ as Savior.

Finally, studying the subject of the afterlife will show us that justice will eventually prevail in the universe when God rights the wrongs on judgment day. Therefore, all accounts will be eventually settled fairly and righteously. The wrongs in this life will be made right.

Therefore, we find that the study of death, dying, and the afterlife is not merely an academic exercise. It has enormous practical value. Indeed, it lays the foundation as to how we should live a life that is pleasing to God in light of the eternity which we all are facing.

QUESTION 2

Where Did Death Come From? If God Created A Perfect World Why Is There Death And Dying?

One of the problems that believers in the God of Scripture face is the explanation of the origin of death. If the God of the Bible is a good God, then why do people die? Do we die because He is not a good God?

Perhaps He is a good God who cannot do anything about the problem of death and dying. In other words, He lacks the ability to deal with it. So which is it? Is God not good or is God not all-powerful?

Actually, neither is the case. God is a good God and He is also all-powerful.

Why then do people die? The Bible gives us the answer. It is because that the human race made choices which brought about death and dying. In fact, it was never God's original intention for us. We can only discover this by an examination of the first three chapters of Genesis.

THE BIBLICAL EXPLANATION OF DEATH

The Bible has much to say concerning the subject of death. It tells us how death originated, as well as how and why it is passed on. From Scripture, we can discover the following truths about death and its origin.

1. THERE WAS AN ORIGINAL PARADISE

The Bible says that the heavens and earth were a direct result of the supernatural creation by an All-Powerful God, the only God who exists. The crown of God's creation was humanity, man and woman.

While in the creation stories of many ancient cultures the formation of the human race was basically an afterthought of the gods, in the biblical account we are the highlight or the crown of His creation. The Bible describes it this way.

> Then God said, "Let Us make man in Our image, according to Our likeness; let them have dominion over the fish of the sea, over the birds of the air, and over the cattle, over all the earth and over every creeping thing that creeps on the earth." So God created man in His own image; in the image of God He created him; male and female He created them (Genesis 1:26-27 NKJV).

Humans have been made in the image of God. This means we have certain characteristics in common with God. For example, like God, we are personal beings who can give and receive love. In addition, we can have a relationship with Him. In other words, we are special to God.

The second chapter of Genesis gives further details on the creation of Adam, the first man. It has this to say about how Adam was made.

> Then the Lord God formed the man of dust from the ground and breathed into his nostrils the breath of life, and the man became a living creature (Genesis 2:7 ESV).

Adam was specially created by God. Indeed, the Lord lovingly formed him from the dust of the ground and breathed life into his lifeless form.

Scripture also tells us about the creation of Eve. We read about the wonderful way in which she was made. The Bible says.

> Then the Lord God said, "It is not good that the man should be alone; I will make him a helper fit for him." Now out of the ground the Lord God had formed every beast of the field and every bird of the heavens and brought them to the man to see what he would call them. And whatever the man called

every living creature, that was its name. The man gave names to all livestock and to the birds of the heavens and to every beast of the field. But for Adam there was not found a helper fit for him. So the Lord God caused a deep sleep to fall upon the man, and while he slept took one of his ribs and closed up its place with flesh. And the rib that the Lord God had taken from the man he made into a woman and brought her to the man (Genesis 2:18-22 ESV).

God created Adam and Eve in His image and placed them in a perfect environment. The Bible says that His entire creation was not just good, it was "very good."

And God saw everything that he had made, and behold, it was very good. And there was evening and there was morning, the sixth day (Genesis 1:31 ESV).

This was a world with no pain, no sickness, and no death. God's world was perfect when He originally created it.

If this is the case, then why do we find an imperfect world with imperfect people? What happened to this perfection?

2. GOD GAVE, ADAM AND EVE, THE FIRST COUPLE, ONE NEGATIVE COMMANDMENT: DISOBEDIENCE WOULD BRING DEATH

The Bible then explains why the world finds itself in its current state. There was only one thing humanity was not allowed to do; to eat from the tree of the knowledge of good and evil. We read in Genesis.

And the LORD God commanded the man, "You are free to eat from any tree in the garden; but you must not eat from the tree of the knowledge of good and evil, for when you eat of it you will surely die" (Genesis 2:16,17 NIV).

The Lord put restrictions upon Adam and Eve that required obedience to His will. God made it clear that disobedience would result in the death of the man and the woman. They would live as long as they remained obedient.

However, if they ate from the forbidden tree the result would be physical death. This involves the eventual separation of the spirit from the body. In fact, they would begin the death process the moment they disobeyed. This was the warning which He gave them.

3. THE SERPENT PROMISED THEY WOULD BE AS GOD IN SOME SENSE

Scripture says that a loving all-powerful God gave humanity the opportunity to choose their own fate. The Bible says, the tempter, Satan, appeared in the form of a serpent in their perfect environment and told them they could be like God if they only would eat from the forbidden tree. Scripture says.

> The snake was sneakier than any of the other wild animals that the LORD God had made. One day it came to the woman and asked, "Did God tell you not to eat fruit from any tree in the garden? . . . God understands what will happen on the day you eat fruit from that tree. You will see what you have done, and you will know the difference between right and wrong, just as God does" (Genesis 3:1,5 CEV).

His promise was a lie. They could never be like God.

4. PARADISE WAS LOST FOR HUMANITY

The Bible says that humanity then fell from their perfect state. Ignoring God's warning, Adam and Eve sinned by eating the fruit. The Book of Genesis explains it this way.

> When the woman saw that the fruit of the tree was good for food and pleasing to the eye, and also desirable for gaining wisdom, she took some and ate it. She also gave some to her husband, who was with her, and he ate it (Genesis 3:6 NIV).

Humans lost that perfect relationship which they had with the Creator. There was now a separation between the Creator and His creation. Adam and Eve began to die the moment they ate the fruit of the tree. While they did not immediately die physically, the death process had started. This process could not be reversed.

5. THERE WAS GOD'S JUDGMENT AS A RESULT

The result of the Fall of Humanity was a series of judgments pronounced by God. This includes the following.

A. THERE WAS JUDGMENT ON WOMEN

The judgment on the woman in general concerned the birth process as well as her submissive role to her husband. The Bible says.

> Then he [God] said to the woman, "You will bear children with intense pain and suffering. And though your desire will be for your husband, he will be your master" (Genesis 3:16 NLT).

The judgment on womanhood was pronounced. Indeed, there would be a number of things they would have to suffer because of the Fall.

B. THERE WAS JUDGMENT ON MEN

The Bible says that God also pronounced judgment upon males as well as females. God made it clear that Adam would have to work on the cursed ground for his food. It would no longer be easy. The Bible puts it this way.

> And to Adam he said, "Because you listened to your wife and ate the fruit I told you not to eat, I have placed a curse on the ground. All your life you will struggle to scratch a living from it. It will grow thorns and thistles for you, though you will eat of its grains" (Genesis 3:17,18 NLT).

Men, like women, received their punishment. The ground would no longer easily yield its food. Life would be difficult from now on.

C. DEATH TO ALL HUMANITY WAS THE RESULT

Not only was the couple banished from paradise, but physical death was now the result. The Lord said to Adam.

> All your life you will sweat to produce food, until your dying day. Then you will return to the ground from which you came. For you were made from dust, and to the dust you will return (Genesis 3:19 NLT).

The punishment went further. While Adam and Eve would experience physical death as a result of their sin, death was also to be passed on to everyone who would be born from then on.

The Apostle Paul would later write.

> Therefore, just as sin entered the world through one man, and death through sin, and in this way death came to all people, because all sinned (Romans 5:12 NIV).

Sin came into being because of the disobedience of Adam. This resulted in death being passed on to everyone because of his original sin.

Paul also wrote to the Corinthians.

> Just as we will die because of Adam, we will be raised to life because of Christ. Adam brought death to all of us, and Christ will bring life to all of us (1 Corinthians 15:21-22 CEV).

Clearly, death is a result of the sin of Adam and it is has been passed on to all of us.

SOME FURTHER OBSERVATIONS TO BE MADE ABOUT DEATH

From Scripture, we can make some other observations about death. They are as follows.

OBSERVATION 1: DEATH IS THE FIRST AND LAST EFFECT OF SIN

Death was not only the first effect of sin, it also is the last thing from which believers are saved. It is our enemy. Paul wrote.

> The last enemy *that* shall be destroyed *is* death (1 Corinthians 15:26 KJV).

Death is indeed our enemy since it is inevitable that all of us will die. However, the good news is that it will someday be destroyed. Therefore, though an enemy, death is a conquered enemy.

OBSERVATION 2: DEATH IS BOTH NORMAL AND ABNORMAL

Depending upon the perspective, death is both normal and abnormal. Death is normal in the sense that it is now the way life ends for fallen humanity. Human beings, who are made from dust, will return to dust. This is the manner in which our world now functions.

OBSERVATION 3: IT IS ABNORMAL: IT WAS NOT GOD'S ORIGINAL INTENTION

There is also the abnormal sense of death. From the account in Genesis, we discover that death is something that is abnormal. In other words, it was never God's original intention or His design. Death came as a result of the choice of the first human pair to commit sin. Humans were created to live, not to die. Death came to the human race as a punishment for sin.

OBSERVATION 4: JUDGMENT WOULD COME AFTER DEATH

In addition, all people are to be judged. The writer to the Hebrews declared the fact that judgment was to come after death.

> People die once, and after that they are judged (Hebrews 9:27 God's Word).

There is a judgment coming after death.

CONCLUSION: DEATH WAS NOT GOD'S INTENTION FOR THE HUMAN RACE

In sum, we can conclude from the biblical evidence that death was not God's original intention; it only came about as a result of the sin of Adam and Eve. Therefore, the God of the Bible is not to be blamed for the way in which our world presently finds itself. Indeed, our world today is not the same world the Lord originally created.

SUMMARY TO QUESTION 2
WHERE DID DEATH COME FROM? IF GOD CREATED A PERFECT WORLD WHY IS THERE DEATH AND DYING?

How can there be death and dying if God is a good God? This is one of the most difficult questions which Christians face. It is usually stated something like this. Either God is not a good God because He allows death and dying, or He is a good God who is not capable or powerful enough of dealing with the death problem.

Therefore, He must be either a weak God or an evil God. Which is it? Is God a bad God or a weak God?

While this is the way the question is usually posed, neither answer is correct. According to Scripture, death came about because of the choice of the first humans. In other words, it was not God who brought death. The biblical evidence is as follows.

In God's original creation, there was no such thing as physical death. Scripture says that the first human beings, Adam and Eve, were the highlight of God's perfect creation. They were made to live forever. Each of them was specially created by God and they were perfect in every aspect. In fact, everything was perfect. Perfect people were living in a perfect world.

Yet there was one negative commandment. God said that they could not eat from the tree of the knowledge of good and evil which was in the midst of Eden. God warned Adam and Eve that disobedience to His commandment would result in their death.

The Bible says that the tempter enticed the woman Eve to disobey God and to eat the forbidden fruit. Adam deliberately disobeyed. After Adam and Eve ate from the tree God then pronounced judgment upon them.

This judgment included physical death. Humans could no longer live forever in these bodies. Adam and Eve immediately began to die. Death was then passed on to all humans as a punishment for the sin of Adam and Eve. Death, therefore, is something abnormal in God's world. God created humans to live, not die.

This is the biblical explanation of the origin of death.

QUESTION 3

Are We Humans Made Up Of Both Body And Spirit Or Are We Merely A Body?

It is important that we understand that we humans are made up of more than just a physical body. The Bible says that we have both a material nature and a spiritual or non-material nature. This non-material part of us is called the "spirit" or the "soul." While the term soul can refer to a number of things in Scripture, it often has the meaning of that non-material part of us, the spirit. Context is always the deciding factor.

Knowing there is a distinction between the body and the spirit, or the soul, will help us understand what the Bible has to say about death, dying, and the afterlife.

From Scripture we learn a number of things about the body and the spirit. This includes the following.

1. THE BIBLE MAKES A DISTINCTION BETWEEN THE BODY AND THE SPIRIT

Scripture says there is a distinction between the human body and the human spirit. In the Book of Job we are told that humans have a spirit within their body. We read.

> But it is the spirit in a man, the breath of the Almighty, that gives him understanding (Job 32:8 NIV).

Therefore, Scripture describes a spirit which is within each of us.

The Bible speaks of God forming the human spirit within us. The prophet Zechariah recorded the Lord saying the following.

> The oracle of the word of the Lord concerning Israel: Thus declares the Lord, who stretched out the heavens and founded the earth and formed the spirit of man within him (Zechariah 12:1 ESV).

The spirit and body are distinct. They can be compared to a house and someone living in the house. The body is the house while the spirit resides inside the house.

Elsewhere Scripture speaks of the spirit living within each of us. The Apostle Paul wrote the following to the church at Corinth.

> For what human being knows what is truly human except the human spirit that is within? So also no one comprehends what is truly God's except the Spirit of God (1 Corinthians 2:11 NRSV).

In another place in the same letter, Paul again makes the distinction between body and spirit.

> For you were bought at a price; therefore glorify God in your body and in your spirit, which are God's (1 Corinthians 6:20 NKJV).

According to Scripture, the spirit lives within the body.

2. THE HISTORY OF CREATION ILLUSTRATES THIS TRUTH

We find further evidence of this from the history of creation. The Bible says that God formed the first human, Adam, from the dust of the earth and then breathed the breath of life into him. We read about this in the second chapter of the Book of Genesis. It says.

Then the Lord God formed the man of dust from the ground and breathed into his nostrils the breath of life, and the man became a living creature (Genesis 2:7 ESV).

We note that this was a two-step process.

First, the body of the man, Adam, was formed from the dust of the ground.

Second, God then breathed into him the breath of life. Only at that time did Adam become a living being. This shows that the spiritual nature, or non-physical nature, is distinct from the physical nature.

When Adam was first formed he was merely a human body without life. It was not until the spirit came into his body that Adam became alive.

Indeed, as James would later write, the body without the spirit is dead. He put it this way.

For as the body apart from the spirit is dead, so also faith apart from works is dead (James 2:26 ESV).

Consequently, the united testimony of Scripture is that we humans are made up of more than just a material body. We have a spiritual component also.

As we will see, it is this spiritual component that will exist forever; either in the presence of the Lord or outside of His presence.

SUMMARY TO QUESTION 3
ARE HUMANS MADE UP OF MORE THAN JUST A BODY?

God has made human beings with a body and a "spirit" which is sometimes called the "soul." In other words, there is a material part of us, the body, as well as an immaterial part of us, the spirit or soul.

This is illustrated in the creation of the first human being, Adam. He was made up of both body and spirit. His body was first formed and then God breathed into his lifeless body the breath of life. At that time he became alive.

The remainder of Scripture testifies to the fact that we have this material part of us as well as this immaterial part of us.

This is an important starting point for us to understand what the Bible has to say about death, dying, and the afterlife.

QUESTION 4

According To The Bible, What Is The Meaning Of Physical Death?

No matter what our status in life, rich or poor, young or old, sooner or later our bodies will cease to function, we will die. The frequency rate of death has been the same from the beginning; one person, one death. Nothing can keep this from happening to us. Nothing.

As we are all aware, death brings pain to everyone. It does not matter what words are said over the dead body, or how normal the corpse looks when it is all dressed up. When someone has been lost, we ask ourselves, "What happens next?"

Consequently, it is important that we discover what the Bible, God's authoritative Word, says about this subject.

From a study of Scripture, there are a number of important things which we can learn about this subject of death.

1. THE BIBLE EMPHASIZES THAT THIS LIFE IS ONLY TEMPORARY

To begin with, Scripture recognizes that this life is only temporary. We do not have that many days in this world. The psalmist wrote.

> Show me, O LORD, my life's end and the number of my days; let me know how fleeting is my life (Psalm 39:4 NIV).

Life is described as fleeting. Indeed, all of us are only here for a brief moment.

In another place we read how temporary life is. The psalmist explained it this way.

> As for mortals, their days are like grass; they flourish like a flower of the field; for the wind passes over it, and it is gone, and its place knows it no more (Psalm 103:15,16 NRSV).

This life is short. There is no doubt about it.

2. THE MAIN IDEA BEHIND DEATH IS SEPARATION

As we noted in the previous question, we humans are made up of both body and spirit. In the Bible, the main idea behind the word "death" is "separation." Thus, physical death, in the biblical sense, is the separation of the spirit from the body.

For example, Adam's natural life began with the union of the body and the spirit. His death was the separation of the two. Whenever physical death is spoken of in Scripture, it has the same idea, the separation of the spirit from the physical body.

God spoke of Adam's body returning to dust. We read the following in Genesis.

> By the sweat of your brow, you will produce food to eat until you return to the ground, because you were taken from it. You are dust, and you will return to dust (Genesis 3:19 God's Word).

The body, which is made up of dust, will return to dust. The remainder of Scripture teaches the same truth; physical death is the separation of the body from the spirit.

THE SPIRIT DEPARTS FROM THE BODY IN DEATH

The Bible consistently testifies that death is the giving up, or the departure of, the spirit from the body. Luke records this happening to Jesus the moment of His death. He wrote.

> Jesus called out with a loud voice, "Father, into your hands I commit my spirit." When he had said this, he breathed his last (Luke 23:46 NIV).

Jesus committed His spirit to the Lord. In other words, He willingly gave it up so that He could die.

THE SPIRIT RETURNS TO THE BODY IN A RESUSCITATION

Another biblical example, that death is the departure of the spirit from the body, can be found in the raising of Jairus' daughter. This young girl had just died when the Lord Jesus came to bring her back to life. We should note that this was a resuscitation or a re-animation of her lifeless body. The Bible explains what happened in this manner.

> So He took her by the hand and called out, "Child, get up!" Her spirit returned, and she got up at once. Then He gave orders that she be given something to eat (Luke 8:54,55 HCSB).

The Bible describes her coming back to life as "her spirit returning to her." This is another illustration of death as the departure of the spirit, the non-material part of us.

The Book of James makes this abundantly clear. James wrote how the body and the spirit work together.

> For as the body without the spirit is dead, so faith without works is dead also (James 2:26 NKJV).

Thus, the spirit leaves the human body at death.

3. DYING BEGINS IMMEDIATELY

It is interesting to note that from the moment we are born, we begin to die. Indeed, the human body is described as a body of death. Paul wrote to the Romans.

> Wretched man that I am! Who will rescue me from this body of death? (Romans 7:24 NET)

Our bodies are characterized by death. In fact, they are in the midst of dying.

4. DEATH IS A PROCESS

Sometimes in Scripture death is looked at as a process. In other words, it is not something that comes upon us suddenly or unexpectedly. Indeed, it is the end of the long process of the wilting and the decay of our mortal bodies.

Consequently, it is spoken of as the gradual weakening of the body. This weakening ultimately ends in death, the cessation of bodily functions.

The Apostle Paul explained it this way in his first letter to the church in Corinth.

> So death is at work in us, but life in you. . . So we do not lose heart. Even though our outer nature is wasting away, our inner nature is being renewed day by day (2 Corinthians 4:12,16 NRSV).

Death is a process that is working in all of us. Indeed, from the moment we are born the process begins to take place.

5. DEATH IS AN ENEMY

Physical death, the separation of the body from the spirit, is described in Scripture as an enemy of humanity. Paul wrote to the Corinthians with the following description of death.

The last enemy *that* shall be destroyed *is* death (1 Corinthians 15:26 KJV).

Death is an enemy of humanity. We can all testify to this!

6. IT IS THE END OF LIFE AS FAR AS HUMANS KNOW

As far as human knowledge is concerned, death is the end of all life and existence for that person. It is the place of no return.

We read about this in Ecclesiastes. It says.

> For the living know that they will die, but the dead know nothing; they have no further reward, and even the memory of them is forgotten . . . Whatever your hand finds to do, do it with all your might, for in the grave, where you are going, there is neither working nor planning nor knowledge nor wisdom (Ecclesiastes 9:5,10 NIV).

As far as we can observe from our human vantage point the dead do not know anything, neither are they able to accomplish anything else here upon the earth.

In the Book of Job, we read the following description of what happens to the dead.

> Just as a cloud dissipates and vanishes, those who die will not come back. They are gone forever from their home--never to be seen again (Job 7:9,10 NLT).

As far as this world is concerned, the dead are gone forever. We know that they will never return to us in this life.

The Old Testament character Job also made this statement about what happens when a person dies. He said.

> Before I go, never to return, to the land of gloom and deep darkness (Job 10:21 NRSV).

Again we note, as far as this life is concerned, death is a land of "no return."

Consequently, if there is any type of conscious existence after death, the answer has to come from some other source than human reason or observation. Indeed, it must come from divine revelation. Undeniably, from mere human observation death is a depressing and frightful subject.

The good news is that divine revelation from the Living God, the Bible, does provide the answer to what happens after the spirit leaves the body. There is something beyond this life! There is a conscious existence on "the other side."

SUMMARY TO QUESTION 4
WHAT IS PHYSICAL DEATH?

In Scripture, the main idea behind death is separation. Physical death is the separation of the spirit from the body. A person dies when their spirit leaves their body.

The first human being, Adam was made up of both body and spirit. His body was first formed and then God breathed into his lifeless body the breath of life. At that time he became alive. When the spirit leaves or separates from the body, then physical death occurs.

After the sin of Adam and Eve judgment was pronounced upon the human race. This punishment included physical death. Adam was told that his body, which was made of dust, would one day return to dust. Because sin has now entered our world, this process of dying begins at the moment we are born.

While physical death is an enemy of humanity it is an inescapable fact, something we all must face. All of us will die.

In addition, as far as we can tell from a human perspective, death ends everything. Life is over and that dead person no longer exists.

Consequently, if there is such a thing as life after death the answer must come from somewhere other than human observation.

Fortunately, we do have the authoritative answers to questions about life after death. These answers are found in the Scripture and the Scripture alone. Consequently, from a study of the Word of God, we will discover that death will hold no ultimate fear for the believer.

What Different Terms Does The Bible Use To Describe Physical Death?

Death is a reality. There is no denying it. The fact of physical death is described in a number of different ways by the writers of Scripture. They are as follows.

1. DEATH IS BREATHING ONE'S LAST

One dies when they "breathe their last." We read of this in the Book of Genesis in the description of the death of Ishmael, the oldest son of Abraham. The Bible says.

> Altogether, Ishmael lived a hundred and thirty-seven years. He breathed his last and died, and he was gathered to his people (Genesis 25:17 NIV).

The end of life is when we take our last breath.

2. THE DEAD HAVE BEEN GATHERED TO THEIR PEOPLE

When the patriarch Jacob died, he is said to have been, "gathered to his people." This description is also found in Genesis. The Bible says.

> When Jacob had finished instructing his sons, he drew his feet into the bed and died. He was gathered to his people (Genesis 49:33 HCSB).

Death is equated to gathering to ones people.

3. THE DEAD GIVE UP THEIR SPIRIT

When Jesus died, the Bible says, "He gave up His spirit." This is the description of His death as recorded in the Gospel of John. It says.

> When Jesus had received the sour wine, he said, "It is finished," and he bowed his head and gave up his spirit (John 19:30 ESV).

The spirit leaves the body at death. In the case of Jesus, He willingly gave it up.

4. THE DEAD PUT OFF THEIR TENT

Peter spoke of his death as the "putting off of a tent." He wrote this description in his second letter as he was about to die. He described his death as follows.

> Knowing that shortly I *must* put off my tent, just as our Lord Jesus Christ showed me (2 Peter 1:14 NKJV).

The tent of flesh is put off at death.

5. THE DEAD WITHER OR FADE AWAY

A graphic depiction of death is given to us in the Book of Job. In this instance, death is spoken of as "withering away" or "fading away." We read.

> He comes forth like a flower and fades away; He flees like a shadow and does not continue (Job 14:2 NKJV).

Withering, or fading, away like a flower is the analogy used of death. It is a picture which all of us can understand. In addition, he also used the analogy of a shadow that does not continue. This is another graphic image of death.

6. DEATH IS GOING DOWN INTO SILENCE

The psalmist spoke of death as "going down into silence." He wrote.

> The dead do not praise the LORD, nor do any that go down
> into silence (Psalm 115:17 NRSV).

The dead are silent. Indeed, we hear nothing further from them. We go into this mode of silence when we die and we are never heard from again in this life.

7. DEATH IS THE WAY OF NO RETURN

Job spoke of his death as going on a "journey where there is no return." In this life, there is no returning from the dead. Once we are dead we remain dead. Thus, we have this description of death.

> For when a few years have come I shall go the way from
> which I shall not return (Job 16:22 ESV).

There is no return from death for any of us. Physical life is over.

8. GOD REQUIRES THE SOUL AT DEATH

In a parable that Jesus gave, He spoke of death as "God requiring the soul." In Luke's gospel we read our Lord saying the following.

> But God said to him, 'Fool! This night your soul is required
> of you, and the things you have prepared, whose will they be
> (Luke 12:20 ESV).

God requires the soul, or demands the life, of the person who dies. We should also note that in this story it is God Himself who made the decision as to when this particular person was to die.

9. DEATH IS SLEEP

Jesus referred to Lazarus' death as "sleep." We read the following in John's gospel about how his demise was described.

Then he said, "Our friend Lazarus has fallen asleep, but now I will go and wake him up" (John 11:11 NLT).

Death is compared to sleep. This illustrates that there is no understanding of those who have died as to what is happening around them.

10. DEATH IS LIKE WATER SPILLED ON THE GROUND

Death is compared to water being spilled on the ground that cannot be gathered again. This vivid illustration is found in the Book of Second Samuel. It says.

> Like water spilled on the ground, which cannot be recovered, so we must die (2 Samuel 14:14 NIV).

Water that is spilled upon the ground cannot be recovered, it is lost forever. This is how death appears to the living.

11. THE DEAD JOIN THEIR ANCESTORS

Death means going to be with "your ancestors." The Lord gave this illustration to Moses when He told him that his death was impending. The Bible says.

> The LORD said to Moses, "Soon you will lie down with your ancestors" (Deuteronomy 31:16 NRSV).

Moses was to join his ancestors in death. As they were in the grave, so he would be. However, as they were alive in the next world, so he would be also!

12. THE EARTHLY TENT IS DESTROYED IN DEATH

Death is the destruction of the "earthly tent." As we observed, Peter referred to his impending death as the "putting off of his tent." Paul added the word "earthly" in describing our bodies. He wrote.

For we know that if the earthly tent we live in is destroyed,
we have a building from God, a house not made with hands,
eternal in the heavens (2 Corinthians 5:1 NRSV).

Our body is compared to an earthly tent that is only here temporarily.
Like everything else on this earth, it is not meant to last forever.

13. DEATH IS DEPARTING

The Apostle Paul spoke of his death as "departing." He wrote to the
Philippians about his desire to depart and to be with Christ.

I am hard pressed between the two: my desire is to depart
and be with Christ, for that is far better (Philippians 1:23
NRSV).

When one dies they leave or depart the body.

14. THE DEAD RETURN TO DUST

Adam, the first human was told that he would "return to dust." God
said the following to him when he ate of the forbidden fruit.

By the sweat of your brow you will eat your food until you
return to the ground, since from it you were taken; for dust
you are and to dust you will return (Genesis 3:19 NIV).

Man, who was made from the dust, would return to the materials from
which he was created. Dust to dust.

15. DEATH IS SYMBOLIZED AS SOMETHING MATERIAL

Death is symbolized in Scripture as something material. In the Book of
Revelation we read of the following description of death by Jesus. He said.

I am the living one who died. Look, I am alive forever and
ever! And I hold the keys of death and the grave (Revelation
1:18 NLT).

Jesus holds "the keys" to death and the grave. Since death is described here as something material, in the future, it will be able to be thrown into the lake of fire.

> Then Death and Hades were thrown into the lake of fire. This is the second death, the lake of fire (Revelation 20:14 NRSV).

There will come a time when death will cease to be.

These various illustrations of death and dying give us an idea of what the end of life meant as far as the biblical writers were concerned.

CONTEXT, CONTEXT, CONTEXT

There is something which we must appreciate. Each of these statements must be considered in their immediate context. Consequently, we must recognize that, at times, the perspective is from an observational point of view. In other words, it looks at death from the viewpoint of those still living. To those of us who are living, death looks like the end. Accordingly, it looks like the dead are forever gone.

However, the biblical teaching is that death is not the end. Indeed, there is life after death. Therefore, let us not make the mistake of seeing these verses in isolation and then concluding that the Bible teaches that death is the end of all existence. It is not. Scripture is clear on this fact. After death every human being will go to one of two destinations. They will either be eternally in the wondrous presence of the Lord or they will be forever separated from Him. There is no third option.

SUMMARY TO QUESTION 5
WHAT DIFFERENT TERMS DOES THE BIBLE USE TO DESCRIBE PHYSICAL DEATH?

The Bible recognizes the fact that human beings will die. Indeed, we live in a fallen world which has been judged by God and one of the judgments is physical death. Consequently there are a number of different descriptions of death found in the Word of God.

They include such phrases as breathing ones last, being gathered to their people, giving up the spirit, withering away, going down in silence, going the way of no return, God requiring the soul, like water falling on the ground, the earthly tent destroyed, departing, sleep, and returning to dust.

Each of these descriptions gives us a vivid picture of the biblical perspective of death.

We must recognize that, at times, the perspective is that of a human observer. Consequently, it looks at death from the vantage point of those still living. To those of us who are living, death looks like the end of all existence. However, in other instances, we have the divine viewpoint of death; death is not seen as the end. In fact, there is an existence beyond the grave for everyone. This is the biblical teaching on the subject.

Therefore, when we read the different descriptions the Bible gives us of death, we must be careful to understand the perspective of the writer. What is he saying in that particular context? This will avoid any confusion on our part of attempting to determine what the Bible teaches about this important subject.

QUESTION 6

Can The Spirit, Or Soul, Be Destroyed?

As we have observed, the Bible teaches that human beings are made up of both body and spirit. Life begins when the two are united, and life ends when the two are separated.

What about the immaterial part of humans? As we mentioned, the Bible sometimes calls it "the spirit" and other times refers to it as "the soul." Can this part, known as the spirit or the soul, die? Does the soul become extinct upon death?

The Bible has much to say about this issue. We can make the following important observations.

THE BIBLE SAYS THE IMMATERIAL PART CANNOT BECOME NONEXISTENT

From the first page of the Bible until the last, Scripture consistently teaches that humans have an immaterial part that will last forever. It is not possible for the soul, or spirit, to become nonexistent.

Indeed, according to Scripture life and death should not be seen as existence and non-existence. Death is simply a transition to a different mode of existence. Therefore, life and death should be viewed as two different states or existence.

We will cite just a few examples of the biblical teaching on the subject.

WHAT THE OLD TESTAMENT SAYS ABOUT THE DEATH OF THE SPIRIT OR SOUL

First, we will look at what the Old Testament says about the death of the spirit or the soul. This is the foundational biblical teaching on the subject.

1. JUDGMENT WAS PRONOUNCED UPON ADAM

When judgment was pronounced upon Adam for sinning against the Lord, it was his body that was judged to go back to its original elements. Scripture says.

> By the sweat of your brow you will eat your food until you return to the ground, since from it you were taken; for dust you are and to dust you will return (Genesis 3:19 NIV).

The spirit, however, was not judged to return to dust because it was breathed into Adam by the breath of God. The body became dust, but the spirit went elsewhere. Never do we find the Bible teaching that the spirit can be annihilated or become extinct. Indeed, it cannot.

2. WE ARE MADE FOR ETERNITY

Scripture teaches that we humans have been made for all of eternity. The writer of Ecclesiastes put it this way.

> He has made everything beautiful in its time. He has also set eternity in the hearts of men; yet they cannot fathom what God has done from beginning to end (Ecclesiastes 3:11 NIV).

One part of us, our soul, has been made to live forever. Death is not the end. Indeed, eternity has been placed in our hearts.

3. THE DISTINCTION BETWEEN BODY AND SPIRIT IMPLIES CONTINUAL LIFE

The distinction that the Bible makes between the body and the spirit is taught in such a way as to imply continual life of the spirit after the body dies. The Bible says.

The dust returns to the earth as it was, and the spirit returns to God who gave it (Ecclesiastes 12:7 ESV).

The spirit will continue to exist, the body does not.

4. THERE IS THE EXISTENCE OF A PLACE OF THE DEAD

The fact that the Scriptures speak of a place where the dead exist shows they have not been utterly annihilated. Isaiah the prophet spoke of the dead in this manner.

The grave below is all astir to meet you at your coming; it rouses the spirits of the departed to greet you--all those who were leaders in the world; it makes them rise from their thrones--all those who were kings over the nations (Isaiah 14:9 NIV).

There is an actual place where the dead reside. They do go somewhere; they do not go out of existence.

5. ENOCH AND ELIJAH DID NOT DIE

Two Old Testament characters, Enoch and Elijah, did not die, but rather went to be with the Lord. In Genesis we read of Enoch.

And Enoch walked with God; and he *was* not, for God took him (Genesis 5:24 NKJV).

Of Elijah, it was said that he did not die. His exit from the earth is described in Second Kings. It says the following.

And as they still went on and talked, behold, chariots of fire and horses of fire separated the two of them. And Elijah went up by a whirlwind into heaven (2 Kings 2:11 ESV).

This certainly implies existence beyond the grave. Since they did not die, something must have happened to them and their bodies. They went somewhere.

Therefore, we have the Old Testament teaching that the immaterial part of humans is not destroyed. It survives beyond this life.

WHAT THE NEW TESTAMENT SAYS ABOUT THE SPIRIT OR SOUL

The New Testament, like the Old Testament also has much to say about those who have died. This includes the following.

JESUS PROMISED ETERNAL LIFE TO THOSE WHO BELIEVE

To those who put their faith in Him, Jesus promised eternal life. We read of a conversation between Jesus and Martha, the sister of the dead man Lazarus. The Gospel of John says.

> Jesus told her, "I am the resurrection and the life. Those who believe in me, even though they die like everyone else, will live again. They are given eternal life for believing in me and will never perish. Do you believe this, Martha?" (John 11:25,26 NLT).

Clearly this speaks of life after this life. Obviously He was not talking about physical death when He said those who believe in Him would never die. All of us do die. Yet there is part of each of us which will never die.

Jesus Said Abraham, Isaac, And Jacob Are Still Alive

In a dialogue with the Sadducees, Jesus spoke of the existence of those who had previously died. Matthew records Jesus saying.

> And as for the resurrection of the dead, have you not read what was said to you by God, 'I am the God of Abraham, the God of Isaac, and the God of Jacob'? He is God not of the dead, but of the living (Matthew 22:31,32 NRSV).

Though Abraham, Isaac, and Jacob had been long dead when God spoke to Moses, God said to him, "I *am* the God of Abraham, Isaac, and Jacob." He did not say "I *was* their God."

According to Jesus, Abraham, Isaac, and Jacob were still living, though they had died physically. Their death upon the earth did not end their existence. This is an early biblical reference to the fact that the dead do not go out of existence. The body dies, but the spirit or soul lives on.

THERE WILL BE JUDGMENT UPON ALL OF HUMANITY

Jesus also spoke of the judgment of the human race. In John's Gospel He spoke of a time when everyone would be judged. He said.

> Do not marvel at this; for the hour is coming in which all who are in the graves will hear His voice and come forth--those who have done good, to the resurrection of life, and those who have done evil, to the resurrection of condemnation (John 5:28,29 NKJV).

If the dead are going to be judged when the graves are opened, then obviously life does not end with physical death. There must be some type of existence beyond the grave if the human race is going to be judged.

THE SPIRIT OR SOUL CANNOT BE ANNIHILATED

The Scripture says the spirit, or soul, cannot be annihilated. While the body may die, the spirit will live on. Death, therefore, is not the end of conscious life. Indeed, it is the separation of the body and the spirit. The spirit, however, lives on in another realm. Therefore, the body is only the temporary residence of humans. Jesus said.

> And do not fear those who kill the body but cannot kill the soul. But rather fear Him who is able to destroy both soul and body in hell (Matthew 10:28 NKJV).

Destroy has the idea of punish, not annihilate. The destruction of the soul means separation from the life of God. Though living, the soul of the unbeliever has no connection whatsoever to God.

5. THERE ARE SOULS UNDER THE ALTAR

The Bible speaks of souls of the dead being under the altar. We read of this in the Book of Revelation. It says the following.

> When the lamb opened the fifth seal, I saw under the altar the souls of those who had been slaughtered because of God's word and the testimony they had given about him (Revelation 6:9 God's Word).

These people still existed after their physical death. This is a further indication that physical death does not end our existence. We will live on after death, all of us.

6. THERE IS A SECOND DEATH

There is a "second death." If death were the end of existence, then why does the Bible speak of the second death of unbelievers? Scripture says.

> Be faithful unto death, and I will give you the crown of life. He who has an ear, let him hear what the Spirit says to the churches. The one who conquers will not be hurt by the second death (Revelation 2:10,11 ESV).

The idea of a second death for unbelievers is another indication that physical death is not the end of existence. A second death assumes there will be a "first death." Therefore, there can be another death after physical death.

MOSES AND ELIJAH WERE AT THE MOUNT OF TRANSFIGURATION WITH JESUS

At the transfiguration of Jesus, Moses and Elijah appeared with Him on the mountain. Matthew records the following.

> And behold, Moses and Elijah appeared to them, talking with Him (Matthew 17:3 NKJV).

This gives further testimony to life after death. Moses had been dead for over a thousand years. Elijah had been taken up in a whirlwind to the presence of the Lord hundreds of years earlier. Yet here they were with Jesus. Obviously they survived beyond the grave.

8. BELIEVERS WILL BE WITH CHRIST

Paul wrote to the Philippians that he wanted to be with Christ. This means he wanted to be with the Lord in the next world. He put it this way.

> I am hard pressed between the two: my desire is to depart and be with Christ, for that is far better (Philippians 1:23 NRSV).

This is another indication of continued existence after death. Paul was assured that if he died he would be with Christ.

9. WE HAVE THE DESIRE TO LIVE FOREVER

The Bible also says that the great saints of Scripture were looking to a better existence beyond this life. The writer to the Hebrews said.

> These all died in faith, not having received the things prom-ised, but having seen them and greeted them from afar, and having acknowledged that they were strangers and exiles on the earth. For people who speak thus make it clear that they are seeking a homeland. If they had been thinking of that land from which they had gone out, they would have had opportunity to return. But as it is, they desire a better coun-try, that is, a heavenly one. Therefore God is not ashamed to be called their God, for he has prepared for them a city (Hebrews 11:13-16 ESV).

Humanity is looking forward to something better; something that God has promised to those who love Him. This promise, however, will not be realized in this present world.

10. NOTHING CAN SEPARATE US FROM GOD

Finally, the Bible says that nothing will separate the believer from the love of God, not even death. Paul wrote to the Romans.

> I am convinced that nothing can ever separate us from God's love which Christ Jesus our Lord shows us. We can't be separated by death or life, by angels or rulers, by anything in the present or anything in the future, by forces or powers in the world above or in the world below, or by anything else in creation (Romans 8:38,39 God's Word).

Nothing means nothing! Not even death! The believer cannot be separated from God. Not now, not ever. Nothing can keep us apart. Therefore, from the totality of Scripture it is clear that the immaterial part of us, the spirit or soul, survives death.

Consequently while death may end our relationships and plans here upon the earth, it is not the end of us. Death is never seen as extinction, nonexistence, or annihilation. Indeed, it is always separation.

Physical death is, therefore, the separation of the spirit or soul from the human body. The body lies in the grave but the spirit lives on. This is what the Bible teaches on the subject.

SUMMARY TO QUESTION 6
CAN THE SPIRIT, OR SOUL, BE DESTROYED?

The Bible says that the body of a human being will return to dust upon death. We were originally made from the ground and we will return to the ground. However, the spirit or soul, which is our real essence, survives. Consequently, the spiritual or immaterial part of us can never die.

According to Scripture, physical life and physical death are two states of existence. They are not to be viewed as states of existence and nonexistence. We still exist whether or not we have died physically. Our spirit survives the grave.

Thus, death in Scripture is always separation; it is never annihilation or non-existence. So our life *never* ends. This is the consistent teaching in both testaments.

Consequently, the Bible can speak of a second death for unbelievers. This implies that physical death is not all that there is. There is life after this life.

Therefore, the spirit or soul can never be destroyed. It will live on for all eternity. This is the message of Scripture from the first page to the last.

In What Sense Do Human Beings Have Immortality?

The Scripture teaches that death is not the end of our existence. The Bible says that the spirit, or soul, of humans will exist forever.

This brings up the issue of immortality. If human beings are going to live forever, does this mean that they are immortal? If humans are immortal, then in what sense do they have immortality? What does the Bible have to say about all of these questions?

The following points need to be made.

1. GOD ALONE HAS IMMORTALITY

Immortality means not subject to death. The Bible says God alone has immortality. In speaking of God, Paul wrote the following to Timothy.

> Who alone is immortal and who lives in unapproachable light, whom no one has seen or can see. To him be honor and might forever. Amen. (Timothy 6:16 NIV).

Another translation puts it this way.

> He is the only one who cannot die. He lives in light that no one can come near. No one has seen him, nor can they see him. Honor and power belong to him forever! Amen (1 Timothy 6:16 God's Word).

In this passage we see that immortality is something that is part and parcel with the nature of God. He alone has it. Angels do not have it, other created beings, such as the cherubim and seraphim do not have it, humans do not have it. The Scripture teaches that only God has life in Himself.

Jesus emphasized this. He said.

> For just as the Father has life in himself (John 5:26 NRSV).

Only God is deathless in His essence. He alone is immortal in this sense of the term. This can be said of no other being in the entire universe.

2. IMMORTALITY IS IMPARTED BY GOD

While God alone has immortality, it is something that He imparts to those who believe in Him. The Old Testament taught that immortality would result by living righteously before God.

We read in the Book of Proverbs.

> In the way of righteousness there is life; along that path is immortality (Proverbs 12:28 NIV).

While God alone is immortal, He can and does impart it to mortals. Only He is able to do this.

THE NEW TESTAMENT TEACHING ON IMMORTALITY

The New Testament also says that God grants immortality to humans who trust in Him. Again, it is emphasized that He alone has the authority to do this.

The Apostle Paul wrote to the Church of Corinth about this subject of immortality. He made the following statements.

> For this corruptible must put on incorruption, and this mortal *must* put on immortality. So when this corruptible has

put on incorruption, and this mortal has put on immortality, then shall be brought to pass the saying that is written: "Death is swallowed up in victory" (1 Corinthians 15:53,54 NKJV).

WE LEARN THREE IMPORTANT TRUTHS

From this passage in First Corinthians, we discover three important things about the subject of immortality.

First, immortality is given only to believers; there is no mention of unbelievers receiving it. Therefore, it is more than endless existence.

Second, it is a gift from God that believers will receive in the future at Christ's coming.

Finally, immortality refers not only to the soul or spirit, but the body is also included. Believers become immortal when this mortal body puts on an immortal one.

We can make some further observations.

A. IMMORTALITY IS BROUGHT BY JESUS CHRIST

God the Son, Jesus Christ, brought immortality to the believer. Speaking of the Lord Jesus, the Apostle Paul wrote the following.

> Who has saved us and called *us* with a holy calling, not according to our works, but according to His own purpose and grace which was given to us in Christ Jesus before time began, But has now been revealed by the appearing of our Savior Jesus Christ, *who* has abolished death and brought life and immortality to light through the gospel (2 Timothy 1:9,10 NKJV).

Jesus Christ brings immortality to mortal humans.

B. WE ARE NOT IMMORTAL BY NATURE

Therefore, according to the Bible, humanity is not immortal by nature. The human soul, or spirit, survives death, but the body does not. Immortality is achieved when the body of the believer is raised and transformed and then united with the soul.

C. WE HAVE AN IMMORTAL INHERITANCE

The Bible also says that Christians have an inheritance that is immortal awaiting them. Peter wrote the following.

> Praise be to the God and Father of our Lord Jesus Christ! In his great mercy he has given us new birth into a living hope through the resurrection of Jesus Christ from the dead, and into an inheritance that can never perish, spoil or fade. This inheritance is kept in heaven for you (1 Peter 1:3-4 NIV)

Note that our inheritance as believers in Christ can never perish, spoil or fade! This promise is for all who trust Jesus Christ. This is one of the wonderful things which await those of us who have believed in Him.

D. IMMORTALITY IS NOT THE SAME THING AS RESURRECTION

We must realize that immortality is not the same thing as the resurrection from the dead. Immorality occurs at the time of the resurrection when the believer receives a new body from the Lord but it is not the same as the resurrection. There is a distinction between the two.

E. IMMORTALITY IS NOT THE SAME AS ETERNAL LIFE

Immortality is not the same as eternal life. Believers receive eternal life the moment they trust Christ. Jesus defined eternal life in this way.

> Now this is eternal life--that they know you, the only true God, and Jesus Christ, whom you sent (John 17:3 NET).

Eternal life consists of a relationship with a person, Jesus Christ. Indeed, eternal life begins the moment we put our faith in Christ.

F. THERE ARE DIFFERENCES BETWEEN GOD'S IMMORTALITY AND OURS

We can sum up the difference between the immortality of God and that of humans as follows. Immortality is basic to the nature of God, not humanity. God is immortal; those humans who believe God's promises have immortality because He gives it to them.

Hence, God is immortal in His essence; believers have a derived immortality. God had no beginning or end. Those humans who have put their faith in the God of the Bible have had a beginning but will have no end. These are some of the differences between us and God.

DO UNBELIEVERS HAVE IMMORTALITY?

If only believers in the God of the Bible have immortality, what can we conclude about the state of unbelievers? Scripture says that unbelievers will exist forever, but they will exist apart from the life of God. They do not have immortality in the biblical sense of the term.

Immortality consists of eternal life in Jesus Christ. Unbelievers have no such life, so they are not immortal according to the biblical understanding of the word. However, they do continue to exist eternally.

SUMMARY TO QUESTION 7
IN WHAT SENSE DO HUMAN BEINGS HAVE IMMORTALITY?

There are a number of things that are important to learn about the subject of immortality.

For one thing, only the God of the Bible is immortal, or deathless, by nature. He is the only immortal being in the entire universe. Angels, as well as other created beings, such as the cherubim and seraphim, are not immortal. Indeed, they all had a beginning. This is primary for us to understand.

While only the Lord has immortality by nature, He, however, imparts immortality to those who believe in God the Son, Jesus Christ. At His return, believers in Christ will receive a glorified, immortal body that will be united with their spirit.

Technically, immortality is not the same as eternal life. Eternal life is received the moment a person trusts Christ as Savior. The Bible says believers presently possess eternal life.

However, our immortality occurs at the resurrection of the body because immortality involves the uniting of the spirit with our new glorified body. Therefore, our immortality is something we will receive in the future.

Such is not the case with those who reject Jesus Christ. Although unbelievers will exist forever, they are cut off from the life of God, and do not have immortality in the biblical sense. Therefore, according to the Bible, immortality is more than eternal existence.

In sum, human beings who believe in Jesus Christ have immortality, unbelievers do not. This immortality is given by the God of the Bible to those who believe in Him. Moreover, it is given by Him alone. He alone has immortality, He alone can grant it to others.

QUESTION 8

What Is Spiritual Death?

Apart from physical death, Scripture speaks of another type of death. This is known as spiritual death. When we examine the Bible, we find out the following about this other type of death.

SPIRITUAL DEATH IS SPIRITUAL SEPARATION

Spiritual death is when a person is alive physically, but dead spiritually. All of us are born spiritually dead or separated from God. The Lord said to Adam.

> But of the tree of the knowledge of good and evil you shall not eat, for in the day that you eat of it you shall surely die (Genesis 2:17 ESV).

Adam and Eve died spiritually at the time that they sinned. In other words, they became different beings than the ones God had originally created. Indeed, their sin separated them from God. They also began to die physically.

2. WE ARE SEPARATED FROM GOD BY OUR SINFUL NATURE

Humanity is now separated from God because of our sinful nature. Jesus talked about what happens to those who have believed in Him, they have passed from death unto life.

> Very truly, I tell you, anyone who hears my word and believes him who sent me has eternal life, and does not come under judgment, but has passed from death to life (John 5:24 NRSV).

Our sins have separated us from a holy God. We are under His judgment unless we receive the forgiveness which Christ offers. Once that happens we pass "from death to life."

Paul says the mind-set or sinful nature of the unbeliever is death. He wrote the following to the Romans.

> If your sinful nature controls your mind, there is death (Romans 8:6 NLT).

Though physically alive and in good health, people, apart from Jesus Christ, are now spiritually dead. It is their fallen sinful nature which controls them.

3. BELIEVERS WERE ONCE SPIRITUALLY DEAD WHILE PHYSICALLY ALIVE

Not only is humanity separated from the Living God by nature, humans are also hostile to Him. The Apostle Paul spoke of believers in the following way.

> Once you were dead because of your disobedience and your many sins. You used to live in sin, just like the rest of the world, obeying the devil—the commander of the powers in the unseen world. He is the spirit at work in the hearts of those who refuse to obey God. All of us used to live that way, following the passionate desires and inclinations of our sinful nature. By our very nature we were subject to God's anger, just like everyone else (Ephesians 2:1-3 NLT).

These believers had been spiritually dead because of their sin. Previously they had lived a life of open hostility to the Lord. Indeed, they followed their own passions rather than following the things of the Lord. That was their past.

4. PAUL SAID HE WAS SPIRITUALLY DEAD

Paul wrote about himself being spiritually dead in the past. He said the following to the Romans.

> At one time I lived without understanding the law. But when I learned the command not to covet, for instance, the power of sin came to life, and I died (Romans 7:9,10 NLT).

Like the rest of us, the Apostle Paul was once spiritually dead.

5. THE WAYWARD SON WAS SPIRITUALLY DEAD

In Jesus' parable, the wayward son was said to have been spiritually dead. In the story the father said the following to the older son.

> We had to celebrate this happy day. For your brother was dead and has come back to life! He was lost, but now he is found (Luke 15:32 NLT).

The son was in a state of spiritual death when he was separated from his father.

6. WIDOWS LIVING FOR PLEASURE ARE SPIRITUALLY DEAD

Paul gives a graphic description of widows who live for the sake of pleasure or self-indulgence rather than living for the Lord.

> But the widow who lives only for pleasure is spiritually dead even while she lives (1 Timothy 5:6 NLT)

Even though they are alive physically, spiritually they are dead.

7. SPIRITUAL DEATH IS A RESULT OF SIN

We again stress what the Scripture teaches. The reason we are all born spiritually dead has to do with original sin. We receive our fallen nature from our parents.

After Adam and Eve sinned, the death sentence was pronounced. All other humans have been born with their sinful nature (the exception to this was the Lord Jesus who was born without sin). Therefore, each of us comes into the world spiritually separated from God. In other words, we inherit a sinful nature.

8. THERE IS A REMEDY FOR SPIRITUAL DEATH

Fortunately, none of us have to remain spiritually dead. When a person trusts Jesus Christ as their Savior they become "born again." This brings the individual into a relationship with God. Jesus said a person must be born again to enter God's kingdom.

> Jesus replied, "I tell you the truth, unless you are born again, you cannot see the Kingdom of God" (John 3:3 NLT).

Therefore, to have any relationship with God we must be born again. There is simply no other way to get to heaven.

The Apostle John stated it simply.

> He who has the Son has life; he who does not have the Son of God does not have life (1 John 5:12 NIV)

Those who have Jesus Christ have life. On the other hand, those who do not have Jesus do not have life. As Scripture emphasizes, they are spiritually dead.

Life or death? It is our choice.

SUMMARY TO QUESTION 8
WHAT IS SPIRITUAL DEATH?

The Bible speaks of the subject of death in a number of ways. One of these ways is known as spiritual death. Since death has the idea of separation, spiritual death is spiritual separation from God. All of us are born spiritually dead, or separated from God. This is because all of us have inherited the sin nature from Adam and Eve.

When this first couple sinned against the Lord they became separated from God in a spiritual sense. They passed their sin nature to the rest of us. The only exception has been the Lord Jesus. Indeed, He had no sin nature and consequently He was not born spiritually separated from God.

This means people can be physically alive and yet spiritually dead at the same time. In fact, the Bible gives a number of illustrations of those who are physically alive yet spiritually dead.

Thus, the spiritual deadness of a person does not impair their physical well-being. They may be in the perfect health yet they are spiritually separated from the Lord.

The only remedy for spiritual death is the new birth which Jesus spoke about. When a person is "born again" by believing in Jesus Christ as their Savior they are no longer separated from God in a spiritual sense. Instead the broken relationship between themselves and the living God has been mended. They are now spiritually alive. Indeed, they will remain spiritually alive for all eternity.

What Is The Second Death, Or Eternal Death?

Physical death is the separation of the spirit from the body. Spiritual death is the separation of human beings from the Lord in a spiritual sense. All of us are born spiritually separated from the Lord, there are no exceptions.

THERE IS A THIRD TYPE OF DEATH

There is a third type of death which is taught in Scripture that is different from spiritual death and physical death. This is known as "eternal death," or the "second death." In the Book of Revelation, we read of this second death. It says.

> He who has an ear, let him hear what the Spirit says to the churches. The one who conquers will not be hurt by the second death (Revelation 2:11 ESV).

Unless spiritual death is reversed in this life, the result will be eternal death or the "second death." This is unending separation between God and all who reject Him. There are several things that need to be understood about the second death.

BELIEVERS ARE NOT AFFECTED BY THE SECOND DEATH

To begin with, believers are not affected by the second death. This wonderful truth is taught in the Book of Revelation. It says.

> Blessed and holy is the one who shares in the first resurrection! Over such the second death has no power, but they will be priests of God and of Christ, and they will reign with him for a thousand years (Revelation 20:6 ESV).

The second death has no authority over those who believe in Jesus Christ. The Lord Jesus has taken upon Himself the punishment which we so richly deserved. Consequently, we do not need to experience the second death. The price has been paid! Therefore, for the believer, there will be no second death.

THE LAKE OF FIRE IS THE SECOND DEATH

The final judgment, or the lake of fire, is the time when the second death occurs. In the Book of Revelation, we read the following.

> And death and the grave were thrown into the lake of fire. This is the second death-the lake of fire (Revelation 20:14 NLT).

The second death is reserved for unbelievers. Those who experience this death are all those whose names are not found written in the Book of Life. The Bible says.

> But cowards, unbelievers, the corrupt, murderers, the immoral, those who practice witchcraft, idol worshipers, and all liars—their fate is in the fiery lake of burning sulfur. This is the second death (Revelation 21:8 NLT).

There is a second death, a second separation, for those who reject Jesus Christ. They are thrown into the lake of fire where they will be forever separated from the Lord.

3. THE SECOND DEATH IS NOT REVERSIBLE; IT IS ETERNAL

Eternal death, or the second death, is the ultimate form of separation. If a person dies in a state of spiritual death, they enter eternity separated from God. This is the second death. Once a person has experienced the "second death" there is no hope for them, it is irreversible.

Therefore, the reality of a "second death" is clearly taught in God's Word. This second death can and should be avoided at all costs.

Trusting Jesus Christ as Savior will keep someone from experiencing the second death. This is the remedy that the Lord offers the human race.

SUMMARY TO QUESTION 9
WHAT IS THE SECOND DEATH OR ETERNAL DEATH?

The Scripture speaks of death in a number of ways. Physical death is the separation of the body from the spirit. Spiritual death, the way in which all of us are born, is the spiritual separation of each of us from God.

Eternal death, or the second death, is the eternal separation of a person from God. If a person does not believe in Jesus Christ in this life then they will experience the second death.

The bad news is that there is no escape from the second death. Once a person is separated from God by the second death they are without hope. Indeed, it is irreversible. They must spend eternity apart from His holy presence. The horrible place is also known as the lake of fire. The biblical description of this place is frightening!

This is why the eternal death or spiritual death is so awful. Fortunately, Jesus Christ has made it possible to avoid the second death. Indeed, He has taken upon Himself the punishment for our sins so that we do not have to suffer. This is the good news of the gospel.

QUESTION 10

Did The Biblical Characters
Bury Their Dead? If So, Then Why?

The Bible has a number of things to say about how ancient Israel, as well as those living at the time of Jesus, dealt with the bodies of those who had died. What we find is a consistent pattern for believers; their bodies were buried.

WHY WOULD THEY BURY THEIR DEAD?

This brings up the question as to why they would do this. Why bury the dead? Once the person is gone from this world there is no returning? Why take the time and trouble to bury them?

From Scripture we can make the following observations about burial practices in biblical times as well as why they buried their dead.

1. BURIAL WAS THE NORM FOR ANCIENT ISRAEL

In the ancient Israel, burial was the norm. When we examine the Scriptures we find that it specifically records the burial of many of the key figures. For example, the burial of the following people are noted in God's Word.

ABRAHAM

Scripture says that the patriarch Abraham was buried upon his death. In fact, God Himself promised Abraham that he would be buried after he had died at a ripe old age. The Bible says.

> As for you, you will die in peace and be buried at a ripe old age (Genesis 15:15 NLT).

Scripture later tells us that Abraham was indeed buried after he had lived to a good old age. We read about this in Genesis. It says.

> Abraham breathed his last and died in a good old age, an old man and full of years, and was gathered to his people. Isaac and Ishmael his sons buried him in the cave of Machpelah (Genesis 25:8-9 ESV).

God's Word, as always, came to pass. Abraham lived to be an old man and after his life had ended his body was buried.

2. BURIAL IN FAMILY TOMBS

We find that Abraham and his descendants were buried in a family tomb.

In fact, before Abraham died he first buried his wife Sarah in the tomb at Machpelah. The Book of Genesis says.

> Then Abraham buried his wife, Sarah, there in Canaan, in the cave of Machpelah, near Mamre (also called Hebron). So the field and the cave were transferred from the Hittites to Abraham for use as a permanent burial place (Genesis 23:19,20 NLT).

We are told that Abraham's son Isaac was also buried.

> Isaac lived a hundred and eighty years. Then he breathed his last and died and was gathered to his people, old and full of years. And his sons Esau and Jacob buried him (Genesis 35:28-29 NIV)

Later we find Jacob, Abraham's grandson who died in Egypt, requesting to be brought back to his homeland to be buried with his ancestors. The Bible says.

Then Jacob instructed them, "Soon I will die and join my ancestors. Bury me with my father and grandfather in the cave in the field of Ephron the Hittite. This is the cave in the field of Machpelah, near Mamre in Canaan, that Abraham bought from Ephron the Hittite as a permanent burial site. There Abraham and his wife Sarah are buried. There Isaac and his wife, Rebekah, are buried. And there I buried Leah.

> It is the plot of land and the cave that my grandfather Abraham bought from the Hittites." When Jacob had finished this charge to his sons, he drew his feet into the bed, breathed his last, and joined his ancestors in death (Genesis 47:28-31 NLT).

Thus, we find the practice of burying the dead in the same family tomb.

3. MOSES WAS BURIED BY THE LORD

The prophet Moses was also buried. Indeed, the body of Moses was actually buried by the Lord Himself! The Bible says.

> So Moses the servant of the LORD died there in the land of Moab, according to the word of the LORD, and he buried him in the valley in the land of Moab opposite Beth-peor; but no one knows the place of his burial to this day (Deuteronomy 34:5-6 ESV).

Again, we have another example of the dead being buried.

4. EXECUTED CRIMINALS WERE BURIED IN THE HOLY LAND

Lest we think that burial was reserved for the wealthy or the righteous, the Bible says that a common criminal deserved to be buried immediately upon death. We read the following command of the Lord in the Law of Moses.

> And if a man has committed a crime punishable by death and he is put to death, and you hang him on a tree, his body

shall not remain all night on the tree, but you shall bury him the same day, for a hanged man is cursed by God. You shall not defile your land that the LORD your God is giving you for an inheritance (Deuteronomy 21:22-23 ESV).

Even someone put to death for their crime deserved immediate burial. In fact, lack of burial would defile the Promised Land. Therefore, everyone who died in the Holy Land was to be buried immediately.

LACK OF IMMEDIATE BURIAL WAS A SIGN OF JUDGMENT

We also find that lack of a speedy burial upon death was looked upon as a sign of judgment. For example, the two men who murdered Saul's son Ish-bosheth were judged harshly by King David. The Bible records what happened to them as follows.

So David gave orders to the young men, and they killed Rechab and Baanah. They cut off their hands and feet and hung their bodies by the pool in Hebron, but they took Ish-bosheth's head and buried it in Abner's tomb in Hebron (2 Samuel 4:12 HCSB).

Thus, the lack of immediate burial was seen as a type of judgment. Although not stated, we assume these murderers were eventually buried. However, note the contrast between these killers and the murder victim Ish-Bosheth. What was left of his body was immediately buried.

5. THERE WAS SECONDARY BURIAL OR SECONDARY DEPOSITION

Tombs in the ancient world were re-used. The ancients would practice what is known as secondary burial or secondary deposition. Upon death, the dead would be laid out on a bench, a cut out area in the family tomb.

After about a year the flesh would decompose. At that time the bones would be taken away from the burial bench and would be placed with the bones of those who previously had died. This would also allow space for the body of the next person who had died to receive the proper burial. This practice would continue for generation after generation.

6. A NEW PRACTICE EMERGED: THE BURIAL BOX

After the end of the Babylonian captivity in 536 B.C. a new practice emerged. Instead of placing the bones of the deceased in some corner of the tomb after the flesh had decomposed, the Jews put the bones in a burial box called an "ossuary." This practice continued to the time of Christ as well as afterward.

Therefore, the evidence is that burial was the normal practice for people in Israel during the Old Testament period. Indeed, whoever died in the Promised Land was supposed to be buried.

7. NEW TESTAMENT BURIAL PRACTICES

This practice continued at the time of Jesus. In the first century, we know that the Jewish people buried their dead. In fact, the burial took place on the day that they died. If the death occurred late in the day or at night, then the person was buried the following day.

THE ILLUSTRATION OF THE SON OF THE WIDOW OF NAIN

This knowledge helps us understand the emotions that would have been raw at the time of burial since the death had just occurred. It also helps us appreciate the situation when Jesus met a funeral procession at the city of Nain. The Bible says.

> A funeral procession was coming out as he approached the village gate. The young man who had died was a widow's only son, and a large crowd from the village was with her (Luke 7:12 NLT).

Since her only son had just died, either that day or the evening before, the emotions of this widow were obviously at their highest. We can only imagine the joy that woman experienced when Jesus brought her son back to life.

THE DAUGHTER OF JAIRUS

There is also the episode of the frantic father, Jairus, whose daughter was near death. He requested Jesus to hurry to his home as his daughter was dying. When the Lord arrived, the girl had died, and the funeral process was already under way. We read.

> When Jesus entered the ruler's house and saw the flute players and the disorderly crowd (Matthew 9:23 NET)

They were already mourning her loss. We find that the flute players were playing a funeral lament by the time Jesus had arrived.

This further illustrates that burial was immediate upon death. As was the case with the previous illustration, the Lord also brought this young girl back to life.

LAZARUS

We find that Lazarus, the friend of Jesus, was buried upon his death. The Gospel of John records the following.

> When Jesus arrived, He found that Lazarus had already been in the tomb four days (John 11:17 HCSB).

We also learn that his hands and feet had been bound with strips of linen cloth and his face wrapped in a cloth. When Jesus brought Lazarus back from the dead He ordered the people to unbind Lazarus. The Bible explains it this way.

> The man who had died came out, his hands and feet bound with linen strips, and his face wrapped with a cloth. Jesus said to them, "Unbind him, and let him go" (John 11:44 ESV).

This account provides us further information of the burial practices of the biblical characters in New Testament times.

ANANIAS

We also read that the body of Ananias, the man who lied to Simon Peter about the price he received for the land he sold, was also wrapped and buried.

> When Ananias heard these words he collapsed and died, and great fear gripped all who heard about it. So the young men came, wrapped him up, carried him out, and buried him (Acts 5:5-6 NET)

Notice that the burial was immediate. Again, this is consistent with what we know of first century Jewish burial practices.

DORCAS

The woman Dorcas, who was a valuable person to the early church, had her body washed and prepared for burial.

> Now in Joppa there was a disciple named Tabitha (which in translation means Dorcas). She was continually doing good deeds and acts of charity. At that time she became sick and died. When they had washed her body, they placed it in an upstairs room (Acts 9:36-37 NET).

However, she was not buried at that time because Simon Peter, by the miraculous power of the Lord, brought her back to life.

JESUS

All four gospels make it clear that Jesus Himself was buried. The Gospel of John gives us some information about what happened to His body upon death.

> After these things Joseph of Arimathea, who was a disciple
> of Jesus, but secretly for fear of the Jews, asked Pilate that he
> might take away the body of Jesus, and Pilate gave him per-
> mission. So he came and took away his body. Nicodemus also,
> who earlier had come to Jesus by night, came bringing a mix-
> ture of myrrh and aloes, about seventy-five pounds in weight.
> So they took the body of Jesus and bound it in linen cloths
> with the spices, as is the burial custom of the Jews. Now in
> the place where he was crucified there was a garden, and in
> the garden a new tomb in which no one had yet been laid. So
> because of the Jewish day of Preparation, since the tomb was
> close at hand, they laid Jesus there (John 19:38-42 ESV).

This provides us with even more detail about the burial practices in New Testament times.

It is clear that Jesus was buried. In fact, the burial of Jesus is stated as part of the gospel message. The Apostle Paul wrote the following to the church in Corinth.

> For I delivered to you as of first importance what I also
> received: that Christ died for our sins in accordance with
> the Scriptures, that he was buried, that he was raised on the
> third day in accordance with the Scriptures (1 Corinthians
> 15:3-4 ESV).

We could add to this that the burial of John the Baptist, as well as the martyr Stephen is also recorded for us in the New Testament.

Therefore, as we look at both testaments we find that burial of the dead was the custom for those who had died.

WHY BURIAL?

We have found that in both testaments burial was the norm for those who were from the nation of Israel as well as for those who placed their faith in Jesus Christ. But why is this so? Why did they bury their dead? There are a couple of stated reasons.

REASON 1: THE LAND WAS NOT TO BE DEFILED

Burial served a number of purposes. For one thing, Scripture says Israel was to bury their dead so that the land would not be defiled. We saw this earlier that even criminals were to be buried. Indeed, they were not to be left hanging on a tree so as not to defile the Promised Land.

In addition, in the future war of Gog and MaGog, we find that the land is to be cleansed from the dead corpses that fall. We read.

> People will be continually employed in cleansing the land. They will spread out across the land and, along with others, they will bury any bodies that are lying on the ground. After the seven months they will carry out a more detailed search. As they go through the land, anyone who sees a human bone will leave a marker beside it until the gravediggers bury it in the Valley of Hamon Gog, near a town called Hamonah. And so they will cleanse the land (Ezekiel 39:14-16 NIV).

This further illustrates the consistent teaching of the Bible; those who die in the Promised Land, the land of Israel, are to be buried. This is true whether the dead are believers or unbelievers. Everyone is to be buried. This is what the Lord specifically commanded for those who died in His Land, the Promised Land! This has been true in the past and it will also be true in the future.

REASON 2: THE PROMISE OF THE RESURRECTION OF THE BODY

In addition, burial illustrated the promise that the dead would some-day rise. While the body was asleep in the grave, the spirit was with the Lord. In other words, it was a sign that they believed in a future resurrection of the body.

However, the body would not always remain in the grave. A day would come when the dead would rise up out of their graves and the body and the spirit would be re-united. The righteous dead would then receive all the wonderful things God has promised them. Burial anticipated that great day which was to come!

THE BOOK OF DANIEL RECORDS THIS PROMISE.

> At that time Michael, the archangel who stands guard over your nation, will arise. Then there will be a time of anguish greater than any since nations first came into existence. But at that time every one of your people whose name is written in the book will be rescued. Many of those whose bodies lie dead and buried will rise up, some to everlasting life and some to shame and everlasting disgrace. Those who are wise will shine as bright as the sky, and those who lead many to righteousness will shine like the stars forever (Daniel 12:1-3 NLT)

We find the same truth stated in the New Testament. The Apostle Paul wrote the following to the Corinthians about the burial of the body and the resurrection of the dead.

> But someone may ask, "How will the dead be raised? What kind of bodies will they have?" What a foolish question! When you put a seed into the ground, it doesn't grow into a plant unless it dies first. And what you put in the ground is not the plant that will grow, but only a bare seed of wheat or whatever you are planting. Then God gives it the new body he wants it to have. A different plant grows from each kind of seed. . . . It is the same way with the resurrection of the dead. Our earthly bodies are planted in the ground when we die, but they will be raised to live forever. Our bodies are buried in brokenness, but they will be raised in glory. They are buried in weakness, but they will be raised in strength. They are buried as natural human bodies, but they will be raised as

spiritual bodies. For just as there are natural bodies, there are also spiritual bodies (1 Corinthians 15:35-38,42-44 NLT)

There is hope for the righteous dead! Indeed, there will come a time when their bodies will be raised from the grave. This is the consistent message of Scripture. Burial of the deceased believer was a way to testify to this wonderful truth!

SUMMARY TO QUESTION 10
DID THE BIBLICAL CHARACTERS BURY THEIR DEAD? IF SO, THEN WHY?

From Scripture we find information about how the believers in the God of the Bible dealt with those who had died. The consistent pattern we find is that the believing dead were buried.

Indeed, the Old Testament records the burial of such figures as Abraham, his wife Sarah, Isaac, and Jacob. They were all buried in the family tomb. Moses was buried by the Lord.

Furthermore, the Bible reveals that burial was the norm for *all* Israelites who died. In fact, we even discover that common criminals who were executed for their misdeeds were also afforded immediate burial. This is another indication of the importance of burial to the people of God.

In the New Testament, we have a number of examples of burial and the burial process. This includes John the Baptist, the son of the widow from Nain, the daughter of Jairus, Lazarus, the martyr Stephen, Ananias, and Dorcas. The most comprehensive account of burial is that of the Lord Jesus.

From these accounts we gain further information about burial practices among God's people. In each and every instance we discover that the dead are buried. There are no exceptions.

As to why the bodies were buried Scripture states that the Lord commanded immediate burial, even for criminals. The stated reason is that His Land would not be defiled. Indeed, this was His Land, the Promised Land!

We find this commanded as far back as the Book of Deuteronomy as well as being illustrated in the future battle of Ezekiel 38 and 39 where the dead corpses are buried "to cleanse the land." Therefore, in the Promised Land, the Land of Israel, whether it may be past, present, or future, the dead are to be buried.

In addition, burial gives us a picture of the biblical truth that someday the spirit will reunite with the body. The dead wait in their graves for the time of their resurrection. This is the realistic hope of all who have believed in the Lord. The burial of the dead illustrated that hope. We find this taught in both testaments.

QUESTION 11

Do We Find Examples Of Cremation In The Bible?

While burial was the norm in the biblical world for those who had died there are a few examples of the bodies of the dead being burned or cremated.

On the one hand, we should note that there is nothing in Scripture which explicitly says that cremation is a sin, or that it is even wrong. However, on the other hand, there is no example of a true believer having their body burned upon death. The evidence is as follows.

CREMATION IS ASSOCIATED WITH JUDGMENT

In Scripture, the norm was burial. The bodies of the dead were not burned. In fact, the burning of a body was often done as a sign of judgment. The Old Testament gives the following three examples.

EXAMPLE 1: THE BODIES OF ACHAN AND HIS FAMILY WERE BURNED IN JUDGMENT

In the Book of Joshua we have the account of a man named Achan. He was the person who disobeyed the commandment of the Lord and took some of the treasure from the conquered city of Jericho. This was in direct violation to what the Lord had explicitly told the people. The Bible describes what happened as follows.

> Then Joshua, together with all Israel, took Achan son of Zerah, the silver, the robe, the gold wedge, his sons and daughters, his cattle, donkeys and sheep, his tent and all that he had, to the Valley of Achor. Joshua said, "Why have you brought this trouble on us? The LORD will bring trouble on you today." Then all Israel stoned him, and after they had stoned the rest, they burned them. Over Achan they heaped up a large pile of rocks, which remains to this day. Then the LORD turned from his fierce anger. Therefore that place has been called the Valley of Achor ever since (Joshua 7:24-26 NIV).

The punishment for his sin was stoning and then the burning of his body. Instead of being buried, he and his family were put to death by stoning and then had their bodies burned for their crime against the Lord. In this case, the burning of the bodies was an obvious sign of judgment.

However, even though their bodies were burned they were not left out in the elements. Note that a pile of rocks covered what was left of them. Again, Scripture is clear that in the Promised Land, the bodies of the dead were not to be left to the elements.

EXAMPLE 2: THE BODIES OF SAUL AND HIS SONS WERE BURNED

The bodies of King Saul, along with his sons, were burned after they had been mutilated by their enemies. Scripture explains what happened in this manner.

> The next day when the Philistines came to strip the slain, they found Saul and his three sons dead on Mount Gilboa. They cut off Saul's head, stripped off his armor, and sent messengers throughout the land of the Philistines to spread the good news in the temples of their idols and among the people. Then they put his armor in the temple of the Ashtoreths and hung his body on the wall of Beth-shan. When the residents

of Jabesh-gilead heard what the Philistines had done to Saul, all their brave men set out, journeyed all night, and retrieved the body of Saul and the bodies of his sons from the wall of Beth-shan. When they arrived at Jabesh, they burned the bodies there. Afterwards, they took their bones and buried them under the tamarisk tree in Jabesh and fasted seven days (1 Samuel 30:8-13 HCSB)

This is not a clear-cut case of cremation as a sign of judgment. The bodies were burned to keep them from being desecrated by the enemies of Israel. They were burned by friends, not enemies. Then they hid the bones by burying them under a tree.

In addition, their bones were eventually collected and buried properly. We read.

So David obtained the bones of Saul and Jonathan, as well as the bones of the men the Gibeonites had executed. Then the king ordered that they bury the bones in the tomb of Kish, Saul's father, at the town of Zela in the land of Benjamin (2 Samuel 21:13-14 NLT)

While Saul was eventually buried, his death was indeed the result of the judgment of God upon him. Saul had rejected the counsel of the Lord and then sought advice from a medium. The fact that his body had to be burned to keep it from being desecrated is also a sign of God's judgment upon him.

EXAMPLE 3: THE BONES OF THE KING OF EDOM WERE BURNED

There is also an illustration of the fate of the King of Edom. The burning of his bones by the Moabites was actually called a "crime" by the Lord. We read the following in the Book of Amos.

The LORD says: I will not relent from punishing Moab for three crimes, even four, because he burned to lime the bones of the king of Edom (Amos 2:1 HCSB).

In this instance, it was a genuine crime to burn the bones of the dead; even that of a pagan king. The Moabites, in point of fact, burned the body to the place where nothing was left, not even his bones.

Therefore, in each instance in which we find a body being burned it always has something to do with the subject of judgment. It is never recorded as the normal means of disposing of a body.

This infers that in ancient Israel cremation was not seen to be an option for the people of God. Unless some type of judgment was involved, the body of the dead was buried.

SUMMARY TO QUESTION 11
DO WE FIND EXAMPLES OF CREMATION IN THE BIBLE?

Cremation is the burning of a dead body rather than burying or embalming it. This was not normally practiced by ancient Israel as a means of dealing with its dead. Those who had died were to be buried. In fact, there are only a few examples in Scripture of someone being cremated.

Furthermore, these examples of cremation are all found in the context of judgment. We find this to be what occurred with an Israelite named Achan. In disobedience to the Lord he took some plunder from the conquered city of Jericho. The judgment he and his family received for the crime was death by stoning and then the burning of the bodies. The burning of their corpses was an obvious sign of judgment. Though burned, their dead bodies were covered with a pile of stones rather than leaving them out in the elements.

The bones of King Saul were also burned. However, this was to keep his body from being desecrated by his enemies. Consequently, this incident cannot be seen as an act of cremation since it was done by friends rather than by enemies. Eventually the body of Saul was properly buried.

The prophet Amos spoke out against the people of Moab for burning the bones of the King of Edom. Even though it was a pagan king, it was considered to be a crime.

In sum, cremation is only specifically condemned in Scripture in the case of the King of Edom. While cremation was rare, we find the actions of the biblical characters in both testaments reveal that it was not seen as an option for those who believed in the God of the Bible. Burial was the proper end for those who had died.

Does The Bible Speak
Of Embalming The Dead?

Today when people die their bodies are either buried or cremated. However, in the ancient world, there was another method of handling the body of one who had departed this earth, embalming. This was particularly true in Egypt where all who could afford it were embalmed after their death.

Yet, this is not true of the nation Israel. In fact, in the entire Bible there are only two examples of people from Israel being embalmed and both of them died in Egypt.

WHAT IS EMBALMING?

Embalming is a process which attempts to preserve the body after death. This consisted of taking out the internal organs and placing the body in embalming fluids for about forty days. This elaborate process was usually performed by a trained group of priests.

The idea behind this process was preparing the body for the afterlife. Egyptians believed the body had to be preserved so that the soul could remain in it.

While this belief was popular in Egypt the Bible teaches no such thing. It is not necessary to preserve the human body so that the soul or spirit will have some place to reside. Scripture teaches that the soul or spirit can exist without the body, but the body cannot live without the soul or spirit. Again, this is another difference between the religion of Israel and that of their pagan neighbors.

JACOB AND JOSEPH WERE EMBALMED

The only biblical characters which were embalmed were the patriarchs Jacob and Joseph. The account of Jacob's embalming is as follows.

> Joseph threw himself on his father, cried over him, and kissed him. Then Joseph ordered the doctors in his service to embalm his father. So the doctors embalmed Israel. The embalming was completed in the usual time-40 days. The Egyptians mourned for him 70 days (Genesis 50:1-3 God's Word).

Here we have the explanation of what happened. Joseph ordered the embalming of his father Jacob upon his death. The Egyptian doctors completed the embalming in a forty day period while Jacob was mourned for seventy days. The body of Jacob was then taken from Egypt to Canaan and buried there.

We should note that the Greek historian Herodotus said that embalming occurred over a seventy day period, not a forty day period. However, Egyptologists have discovered that too much damage would be done to the body if the process was extended to seventy days. The dehydration of the body takes forty days, the exact time Genesis says that the embalming process occurred. Again, the Bible is proved to be exact in its historical reference.

Joseph was also embalmed. The Bible explains it this way.

> Joseph died when he was 110 years old. His body was embalmed and placed in a coffin in Egypt (Genesis 50:26 God's Word).

Like his father, his bones were eventually taken from Egypt to the Promised Land and buried there. We read.

The bones of Joseph, which the Israelites had brought along with them when they left Egypt, were buried at Shechem, in the parcel of ground Jacob had bought from the sons of Hamor for 100 pieces of silver. This land was located in the territory allotted to the descendants of Joseph.(Joshua 24:32 NLT)

WHY WERE THEY EMBALMED?

The Bible does not say why Jacob and Joseph were embalmed. Most likely, it was to appease the Egyptians who may have felt threatened by Joseph's family moving from Canaan to Egypt.

It also served another purpose. Indeed, it preserved the bodies of these two men so that they could eventually be buried in the Promised Land.

Whatever the case may be, they are the only two examples of biblical characters which we are told had their bodies embalmed. The bodies of the believers in the God of the Bible were buried, not cremated or embalmed.

SUMMARY TO QUESTION 12
DOES THE BIBLE SPEAK OF EMBALMING THE DEAD?

Traditionally, bodies of the dead have been dealt with in one of three ways; embalming, burial, or cremation. Scripture gives examples of all three.

Embalming consisted of removing the internal organs and then placing fluids in the body to preserve it. This was performed by people who had special skill in this art. The process was done in Egypt because of the belief that the soul or spirit needed some sort of familiar place to reside in the next world. Therefore, the body was preserved for the afterlife.

This practice, however, was not done in Israel because there was no such belief that the body had to be preserved to be a repository for the spirit or soul in the next life. The spirit, the soul, can live without the body while the body cannot live without that invisible part of us, the spirit, the soul.

Indeed, the only biblical characters who were embalmed were two who had died in Egypt, Jacob and Joseph. Joseph ordered the embalming of his father and was himself embalmed upon death. The embalming of Jacob probably was to serve two purposes.

First, it was to calm the fears of the Egyptians who may have been threatened by the arrival of Jacob and his family in Egypt. The fact that he was embalmed would have calmed those fears.

Second, it allowed his body to be preserved for burial in his native Canaan. The same holds true for Joseph. His body and bones were preserved and eventually taken to the Promised Land hundreds of years later when the nation of Israel made its exodus from Egypt.

In sum, these are the only two examples of biblical characters being embalmed, the two which died in Egypt. For believers in the God of the Bible burial was the proper way to deal with the bodies of the dead.

QUESTION 13

Does The Bible Encourage Superstitious Practices About Death, Dying, And Burial?

In the ancient world there was much superstition surrounding death and the burial of the dead. Indeed, there still remains much superstition in our modern world about this subject.

However, in contrast to the superstitious practices of pagan nations, we find no such practices commanded or condoned in Israel. This is what we should expect if the Bible is what it claims to be; God's divine revelation of Himself to the human race. We note the following.

FOOD WAS NOT SUPPOSED TO BE LEFT IN THE TOMBS FOR THE DEAD

There is no command in Scripture of leaving food in the grave of those who died. While this was practiced by other nations we find no such thing in Israel.

In fact, we find that those in ancient Israel knew of the pagan practice of offering food for the dead but they themselves were commanded not to participate in it. We read the following in Deuteronomy of what the people were supposed to testify to the Lord when they had obeyed His commandments.

> I have not violated or forgotten your commandments. I have not eaten anything when I was in mourning, or removed any of it while ceremonially unclean, or offered any of it to the

dead; I have obeyed you and have done everything you have commanded me (Deuteronomy 26:13-14 NET)

Notice there is the specific mention of offering food for the deceased. The people were explicitly commanded by the Lord not to do this. Consequently they were to testify to the Lord that they had kept His commandments which included not offering food for the dead.

This statement indicates they were aware of the practice but were commanded not to participate in it. Again, this is another example that Israel was supposed to be a unique nation, unlike their pagan neighbors.

ISRAEL WAS UNIQUE

While there have been tombs found in the Holy Land which did have food and other things placed for the deceased it has yet to be clearly demonstrated that these were the tombs of the Israelites. There is no evidence that the people continued to visit the tombs of their dead ancestors and provide food for their loved ones.

Even if it were eventually discovered that some of the people of Israel did leave food for their dead it would have been their adopting the pagan practices of the nations around them. This is something, which we have just seen, that the Lord warned against.

Earlier, in the Book of Deuteronomy, we find a general warning from the Lord to His people.

When you come into the land that the LORD your God is giving you, you shall not learn to follow the abominable practices of those nations (Deuteronomy 18:10 ESV).

Again we stress that Israel was to be a unique nation. They were a special people separated to God. Thus, they were specifically commanded not to adopt pagan practices.

When Israel did adopt the superstitious and pagan practices of their ungodly neighbors these practices were condemned by the Lord and by His prophets.

In sum, we do not find God, or His spokesmen the prophets, commanding anything to His people which could be considered superstitious.

Of course, this is exactly what we should expect from the Bible, the Word of the living God.

SUMMARY TO QUESTION 13
DOES THE BIBLE ENCOURAGE SUPERSTITIOUS PRACTICES ABOUT DEATH, DYING AND BURIAL?

God separated the nation Israel from all the other nations of the world. They were to be His people, a special witness of who He is and what He expects. Therefore, we do not find the same superstitious beliefs and practices about death, dying and burial in Scripture as we find among the ancients.

For example, nowhere do we find the biblical writers ordering the people to leave food for the dead so as to help them on their journey in the afterlife. While other nations thought they were helping the dead with such practices, the biblical writers would have none of this superstition.

In fact, we find just the opposite. In the Book of Deuteronomy the people were supposed to testify to the Lord that they had kept His commandments which included not leaving food for the deceased! This indicates that the people were aware of the pagan practice but that the Lord had specifically commanded them against doing it. Indeed, they were not to follow the practices of the heathen nations.

However, Israel, at times, adopted some of the pagan practices of their neighbors. When this occurred God sent His prophets to roundly condemn such acts. God's people were not to do the same things as the heathens.

To sum up, the biblical teachings on death, dying, burial, and the after-life are unique. They are the result of God's divine revelation not some type of human reasoning or superstition. This is why we find no super-stitious practices encouraged.

QUESTION 14

Does The Bible Command Or Allow Worship Of Ancestors?

One of the popular practices in biblical times was the veneration or worship of dead ancestors. This practice also continues in our modern world. Supposedly these ancestors have some sort of ability to control events in our world. Such a belief has caused the living to fear the dead and thus do whatever is necessary to appease them.

While this belief was widespread in the world of the Bible we find no such idea or practice of ancestor worship commanded in Scripture, or even tolerated.

Though the people of Israel were influenced by their pagan neighbors, and often practiced such superstitious things, the prophets of God condemned such actions in no uncertain terms. The evidence is as follows.

WORSHIP IS TO BE DIRECTED AT GOD ALONE

The Ten Commandments make it clear who we are to worship. Indeed, it is God and Him alone. We read the following.

> And God spoke all these words: "I am the LORD your God, who brought you out of Egypt, out of the land of slavery. "You shall have no other gods before me. "You shall not make for yourself an idol in the form of anything in heaven above or on the earth beneath or in the waters below. You shall not

> bow down to them or worship them; for I, the LORD your
> God, am a jealous God (Exodus 20:1-5 NIV).

Only the God of Scripture is worthy to receive our worship. Indeed, there are no other gods which exist. Therefore, we should direct our worship to Him and Him alone.

The New Testament also makes this clear. When Jesus was tempted by the devil, He proclaimed that God alone is to be worshipped. We read.

> Then Jesus said to him, "Away with you, Satan! For it is writ-ten, 'You shall worship the LORD your God, and Him only you shall serve'" (Matthew 4:10 HCSB).

Jesus emphasized that it is only the God of the Bible who is to be worshipped. Worship of any other thing, whether it is living or dead, or some type of inanimate object such as an idol, was strictly forbid-den. Ancestor worship was thus not an option for the people of God. Neither is it an option today.

THE DEAD DO NOT INFLUENCE THE LIVING

There is something else. According to Scripture, the dead are sepa-rated from the living. They do not contact us or protect us. This is the responsibility of God alone.

Therefore, it is not possible for them to have any influence over us see-ing that they are prohibited from contacting us. This is a further reason why ancestor worship is worthless.

SUMMARY TO QUESTION 14
DOES THE BIBLE COMMAND OR ALLOW WORSHIP OF ANCESTORS?

Ancestor worship was popular in the ancient world and it remains popular in some parts of the world today. The idea behind ancestor worship is that these dead ancestors had certain powers to protect the living. In some mysterious way, they could supposedly insert themselves into the lives of people and protect them from harm.

While some of the people of Israel may have practiced ancestor worship this is strictly condemned in Scripture. The Bible says that God, and God alone, is to be worshipped. We are not to worship the spirits of the dead or suppose they have some type of control over us. There is nothing in the Bible which encourages this sort of practice.

Furthermore, it is clear from Scripture that the dead have no contact with the living. Indeed, this is something which the Bible says that the Lord does not allow. This is a further reason as to why the worship of ancestors can be of no help whatsoever to the people of earth.

QUESTION 15

What Hope Did The Old Testament Give For Those Who Had Died?

While unbelievers try a variety of different ways to face the question of death and dying, in the end, none of them can really help. Fortunately there is a remedy for death.

From the very beginning, the Old Testament has given humanity hope for something better beyond this life. There are a few things which we should note.

THREE GREAT EVENTS WILL OCCUR

The entire Old Testament looked forward to the time when the Lord would come to the earth, raise the dead, judge the world righteously, and then set up His kingdom. Indeed, the people were looking forward to three great events.

EVENT 1: THE LORD WOULD COME AND RAISE THE DEAD

The Bible promised that the Lord would personally come to earth one day. His coming was a major theme of the Old Testament. Upon His return, the dead would be raised.

EVENT 2: HUMANITY WOULD BE RIGHTEOUSLY JUDGED

When the Lord returns, the wrongs committed in this life would be made right. Those who lived in the Old Testament period understood that not all wrongs would be made right in this life. They trusted the Lord would vindicate the righteous and judge the ungodly. There would be a final righting of wrongs when the dead are judged.

EVENT 3: THE RIGHTEOUS WOULD INHERIT GOD'S KINGDOM

After this judgment, the righteous would inherit the kingdom of God and live with Him forever. This is the hope that the Old Testament provided to the believer.

THE OLD TESTAMENT ILLUSTRATES THESE TRUTHS

We find these three great prophetic events illustrated in a variety of ways. They are as follows.

1. ENOCH DID NOT DIE

The earliest specific biblical mention of someone living in the afterlife is Enoch. After Enoch lived a life that was pleasing to God, the Bible says that God took him.

> Altogether, Enoch lived a total of 365 years. Enoch walked faithfully with God; then he was no more, because God took him away (Genesis 5:23-24 NIV)

This implied that Enoch was brought into God's presence. The New Testament agrees with this truth. We read in Hebrews.

> By faith Enoch was taken up so that he should not see death, and he was not found, because God had taken him. Now before he was taken he was commended as having pleased God (Hebrews 11:5 ESV).

Because Enoch went to be with the Lord, he served as an example for others who were to follow. He certainly was not going to be alone in heaven!

Only two Old Testament figures, Noah (Genesis 6:9) and Enoch, are said to have walked with God. Walking with God meant intimate communion with Him. Malachi records God saying.

> True instruction was in his mouth and nothing false was found on his lips. He walked with me in peace and uprightness, and turned many from sin (Malachi 2:6 NIV).

The intimate walking with God continued when Enoch came into God's presence. Therefore we have the idea of continual consciousness and communion with God beyond this life. Although Enoch was not resurrected, he did experience glorification in the presence of the Lord.

2. ELIJAH DID NOT DIE

Elijah, like Enoch, did not die, but went to be with the Lord. The Bible records what happened to this prophet of God as follows.

> "You have asked a difficult thing," Elijah said, "yet if you see me when I am taken from you, it will be yours-- otherwise not." As they were walking along and talking together, suddenly a chariot of fire and horses of fire appeared and separated the two of them, and Elijah went up to heaven in a whirlwind (2 Kings 2:10,11 NIV).

There was no death for either Enoch or Elijah. They were both ushered into the presence of the Lord. This indicated that there was existence after this life.

3. JOB LOOKED FORWARD TO A BETTER LIFE

The Old Testament character Job suffered a tremendous amount of pain, bother personal and physical. Yet, through all his suffering, he still expressed hope that there was something better after this life. We read these great words from him.

But as for me, I know that my Redeemer lives, and he will stand upon the earth at last. And after my body has decayed, yet in my body I will see God! I will see him for myself. Yes, I will see him with my own eyes. I am overwhelmed at the thought! (Job 19:25-27 NLT)

Although Job may not be vindicated in this life, he had a hope for life beyond the grave. He believed that this life was not all that there is.

4. ABRAHAM WAS PROMISED LIFE BEYOND THE GRAVE

From the account of Abraham, we have another testimony to a conscious afterlife for those who have died. Abraham was to be gathered to his people in peace upon his death. God said to him.

But you will die in peace and be buried at a very old age (Genesis 15:15 God's Word).

This eventually came to pass. We read further in Genesis.

Then Abraham breathed his last and died at a good old age, an old man and full of years; and he was gathered to his people (Genesis 25:8 NIV).

This indicates more than being buried in the family tomb. Abraham had left his homeland and went to a new land. His body was not returned to the land of his father's. Indeed, he was buried in the land to which he was promised. The only other person that had been buried in his tomb was his wife Sarah.

Therefore, the phrase "gathered to his people" does not have the idea of burial with his ancestors. In fact, in the entire Old Testament, this phrase is distinguished from the act of burial. Abraham was promised that he would join his people in the next world.

Therefore the expression "to be gathered with his people" does not mean that he was buried in the family tomb. It contains the hope of a reunion with ones ancestors beyond the grave. Others were given the same promise.

> When Jacob finished commanding his sons, he drew up his feet into the bed and breathed his last and was gathered to his people (Genesis 49:33 ESV).

Death was not the end for Jacob. He too went to be with his people in the next world after his earthly life was completed.

When God spoke to Moses in the burning bush He identified Himself as the God of Abraham, Isaac, and Jacob.

> Then he said, I am the God of your father, the God of Abraham, the God of Isaac and the God of Jacob." At this, Moses hid his face, because he was afraid to look at God (Exodus 3:6 NIV).

Note well that the Lord said, "I am" not "I was" the God of Abraham, Isaac, and Jacob. Though long dead, Abraham, Isaac, and Jacob were still alive in God's presence.

THE PSALMS SPEAK OF HOPE BEYOND THE GRAVE

In the Book of Psalms, we find further expressions of a hope beyond the grave. This includes a bodily resurrection.

> No wonder my heart is filled with joy, and my mouth shouts his praises! My body rests in safety. For you will not leave my soul among the dead or allow your godly one to rot in the grave. You will show me the way of life, granting me the joy of your presence and the pleasures of living with you forever (Psalm 16:9-11 NLT).

The psalmist expresses the hope of being in God's presence forever. This is another indication of life beyond the grave.

In another Psalm we read.

> And I--in righteousness I will see your face; when I awake, I will be satisfied with seeing your likeness (Psalm 17:15 NIV).

There is hope for the righteous after this life is over.

A. THE WICKED AND RIGHTEOUS ARE CONTRASTED

In the 49th Psalm we are presented with a contrast between the wicked and the righteous. At the end of their lives, we are told that the wicked are like animals that perish.

> But man, despite his riches, does not endure; he is like the beasts that perish. . . . A man who has riches without understanding is like the beasts that perish (Psalm 49:12, 20 NIV).

The wicked have no hope of living eternally with the Lord. However, they will exist somewhere.

B. THE RIGHTEOUS HAVE HOPE

In contrast, the righteous have hope. Speaking of the believer, the psalmist wrote.

> That he should continue to live eternally, *and* not see the Pit (Psalm 49:9 NKJV).

Eternal life awaits those who have trusted in the Lord.

The psalmist also had hope that he would be freed from the power of death. He expressed the following hope.

> But God will redeem my soul from the power of the grave, for He shall receive me (Psalm 49:15 NKJV).

This is another indication of a genuine hope of life after death. As the Lord received Enoch and Elijah, so will He receive the righteous, the ones who place their trust in Him.

There was also the hope of heaven. We also read in the psalms.

> You will keep on guiding me with your counsel, leading me to a glorious destiny. Whom have I in heaven but you? I desire you more than anything on earth. My health may fail, and my spirit may grow weak, but God remains the strength of my heart; he is mine forever (Psalm 73:24-26 NLT).

We, as believers, do indeed have a "glorious destiny."

Therefore, the Bible contrasts the fate of the wicked with the fate of the righteous. Their destinies could not be more different.

6. DAVID WILL LIVE AGAIN

The Bible specifically says that King David would be raised in the future to feed the flock of Israel. We read of this in the writings of the prophet Ezekiel. It says.

> And I, the LORD, will be their God, and my servant David shall be prince among them; I, the LORD, have spoken (Ezekiel 34:24 NRSV).

This prediction was written hundreds of years after David's death. David, though physically dead, has the promise from God of a future rule in His kingdom.

7. ISAIAH SPOKE OF HOPE BEYOND THE GRAVE

In the Book of Isaiah we read of hope beyond the grave. The Bible says.

> He will swallow up death forever. Then the Lord GOD will wipe away the tears from all faces, and the disgrace of his

people he will take away from all the earth, for the LORD has spoken (Isaiah 25:8 NRSV).

This is an unmistakable prediction of life after this life.

In another place, Isaiah recorded a statement which is even more pertinent to this question. Indeed, this is about as clear as it can be.

> But your dead will live; their bodies will rise. You who dwell in the dust, wake up and shout for joy. Your dew is like the dew of the morning; the earth will give birth to her dead (Isaiah 26:19 NIV).

There is hope beyond the grave for those who have died.

8. DANIEL SPOKE OF THE AFTERLIFE

In the Book of Daniel, we also have hope in the afterlife expressed. He wrote the following about what will occur in the future.

> Multitudes who sleep in the dust of the earth will awake: some to everlasting life, others to shame and everlasting contempt (Daniel 12:2 NIV).

Daniel was promised a personal reward after this life. The angel who had given him this information about future judgments said the following to him.

> As for you, go your way till the end. You will rest, and then at the end of the days you will rise to receive your allotted inheritance (Daniel 12:13 NIV).

There was a belief that there would be life after this life. This is made abundantly clear from these texts.

9. ZECHARIAH SPOKE OF A RESURRECTION

Furthermore, the prophet Zechariah recorded his belief in a resurrection of the dead. He wrote the following.

You will flee through this valley, for it will reach across to Azal. Yes, you will flee as you did from the earthquake in the days of King Uzziah of Judah. Then the Lord my God will come, and all his holy ones with him. (Zechariah 14:5 NLT).

If the "holy ones" in this context refers to believers rather than angels, then we have a guarantee of the resurrection of the righteous.

10. THERE ARE WARNINGS ABOUT CONTACTING THE DEAD

Finally, there are the various warnings in the Old Testament about the living contacting the dead. From the time of Moses the people were warned about dabbling in areas of the occult such as talking to the dead. We read in Deuteronomy.

When you come into the land that the LORD your God is giving you, you must not learn to imitate the abhorrent practices of those nations. No one shall be found among you who makes a son or daughter pass through fire, or who practices divination, or is a soothsayer, or an augur, or a sorcerer, or one who casts spells, or who consults ghosts or spirits, or who seeks oracles from the dead. For whoever does these things is abhorrent to the LORD; it is because of such abhorrent practices that the LORD your God is driving them out before you. (Deuteronomy 18:9-12 NRSV).

These warnings would make no sense whatsoever if the dead ceased to exist. Why warn people about contacting people in the next world if there was no such thing as an afterlife? The fact that they were warned shows they had an early belief of existence beyond this life.

Whether or not they would actually make contact with these people is not the issue. The point is that the dead did not cease to exist.

11. THE EPISODE OF SAMUEL AND SAUL PROVIDES EVIDENCE OF FUTURE EXISTENCE

In First Samuel 28, there is the episode of Saul contacting the spirit of the dead prophet Samuel. No matter how one understands what happened in this account, it does prove that the people assumed the dead lived on in the next world. This is clear from the context of the story.

Consequently, from the totality of the Old Testament evidence, we find that life beyond the grave is indeed a reality. This life is not all that there is. All of us will continue to exist in the next world, in the afterlife.

SUMMARY TO QUESTION 15
WHAT HOPE DID THE OLD TESTAMENT GIVE FOR THOSE WHO HAD DIED?

It is clear that the Old Testament gave people hope for life beyond the grave. Those who had died are regarded as still existing. Indeed, they do not become non-existence upon death. Thus, while death is the end of existence here on earth, it is not the end of all existence.

The Old Testament speaks of a number of coming events which would involve those who had died. The Bible says that the Lord will return to earth, He will raise the dead, judge the people, and set up His kingdom.

From the patriarch Enoch, as well as the prophet Elijah, being taken away to the presence of the Lord, to the statements in Job, the Psalms, Isaiah, and Daniel, the Old Testament gave individuals a hope beyond this life. Those who died had immediate access into the presence of the Lord, He took them to Himself.

In addition, they were all waiting for a future time when their bodies would be raised. While it is clear that these people were still alive in the next world, it is also clear that their bodies were decaying in the grave. The bodies and the spirits had separated.

However, someday these bodies and spirits were to be united in the resurrection of the dead. This is the hope which the Old Testament gave to the people.

The warnings of the Lord that the living should not attempt to contact the dead gives further testimony of existence in the afterlife. The fact that they were warned not to try to reach out to those in the next life makes it clear that they believed deceased people were still alive and conscious.

It was, however, the New Testament, that would reveal a more detailed description of the next world.

QUESTION 16

What Hope Does The New Testament Give For The Dead?

The Old Testament provided a genuine hope for people who had to face death. Because of the sin of Adam and Eve, physical death entered into the world. Individuals were born spiritually separated from God. In other words, they were in a state of spiritual death. Spiritual death eventually leads to eternal death.

There is, however, a remedy for spiritual death. This is the good news, or the gospel, which the New Testament reveals. A person does not have to be separated from God, either in this life, or in the next. Indeed, they do not have to remain spiritually dead. A number of points need to be made.

1. JESUS DIED AS OUR SUBSTITUTE

The hope that the New Testament gives the dead is based upon the Person and work of Jesus Christ. He is the One who has solved the death problem. The Bible says that the death of Jesus Christ satisfied the righteous requirements of God for sin. His death was a substitute on our behalf. In other words, He died in our place. The Bible says.

> For God was in Christ, reconciling the world to him-
> self, no longer counting people's sins against them. This is
> the wonderful message he has given us to tell others. We
> are Christ's ambassadors, and God is using us to speak

to you. We urge you, as though Christ himself were here pleading with you, "Be reconciled to God!" For God made Christ, who never sinned, to be the offering for our sin, so that we could be made right with God through Christ (2 Corinthians 5:19-21 NLT).

Because Christ died on our behalf, humanity does not have to suffer for their sins, and be eternally separated from God. This is the good news of the gospel.

2. BELIEVERS HAVE HAD A NEW BIRTH

Only by the new birth, receiving Jesus Christ as Savior, can a person become spiritually alive. Jesus spoke of the necessity of the new birth to enter the kingdom of God.

> Jesus answered him, "Truly, truly, I say to you, unless one is born again he cannot see the kingdom of God" (John 3:3 ESV).

To enter the kingdom of God one must experience this new birth. Without it, there is no entrance into the Lord's presence in the next life. Those who believe in Jesus Christ have had a spiritual rebirth. We are now "born again" through faith in Him.

3. THERE IS LIFE THROUGH JESUS CHRIST

We also find that belief in Jesus secures everlasting life in the presence of God. There will be no spiritual death for those who have trusted Him. Jesus said.

> Most assuredly, I say to you, if anyone keeps My word he shall never see death (John 8:51 NKJV).

The death we shall never see is spiritual death, spiritual separation from God. Indeed, the believer is now eternally united to Christ through our belief in Him.

In another place, Jesus told the sister of the dead man Lazarus that He Himself was the resurrection and the life! We read of this tremendous statement in the Gospel of John.

> Jesus told her, "I am the resurrection and the life. Those who believe in me, even though they die like everyone else, will live again. They are given eternal life for believing in me and will never perish. Do you believe this, Martha?" (John 11:25,26 NLT).

Jesus is not saying that believers will never die physically. To the contrary, He acknowledges they will experience physical death. However, because He is the resurrection and the life, those who are physically dead will be raised bodily.

4. BELIEVERS ARE NOW SPIRITUALLY ALIVE

Those who have trusted Christ as Savior are dead to sin but alive to God. Paul wrote the following to the Romans.

> So consider yourselves dead to sin's power but living for God in the power Christ Jesus gives you. Therefore, never let sin rule your physical body so that you obey its desires. Never offer any part of your body to sin's power. No part of your body should ever be used to do any ungodly thing. Instead, offer yourselves to God as people who have come back from death and are now alive. Offer all the parts of your body to God. Use them to do everything that God approves of (Romans 6:11-13 God's Word).

God's life is now in us because of Jesus Christ. This spiritual life will never cease.

The Apostle Paul also wrote to the Ephesians about the spiritual life which Christ has provided for us. He said that we are alive together with Christ and seated with Him in heavenly places! He put it this way.

> But because of his great love for us, God, who is rich in
> mercy, made us alive with Christ even when we were dead in
> transgressions--it is by grace you have been saved. And God
> raised us up with Christ and seated us with him in the heav-
> enly realms in Christ Jesus (Ephesians 2:4-6 NIV).

What a tremendous truth this is! There is continuous spiritual life in
Jesus Christ for those of us who have believed in Him.

5. BELIEVERS ARE HEIRS TO GOD

Those who believe in Jesus Christ are heirs to His promises. Paul wrote
about this wonderful news in his letter to the Romans. He put it this way.

> So you should not be like cowering, fearful slaves. You should
> behave instead like God's very own children, adopted into
> his family--calling him "Father, dear Father." For his Holy
> Spirit speaks to us deep in our hearts and tells us that we are
> God's children. And since we are his children, we will share
> his treasures-- for everything God gives to his Son, Christ, is
> ours, too. But if we are to share his glory, we must also share
> his suffering (Romans 8:15-17 NLT).

We will share His destiny. All of the things which belong to Him
belong to us. He has made us heirs to His treasures.

6. EVERYTHING IS NOW OURS

We find this also stated in Paul's letter to the Corinthians Everything
belongs to God's children. Paul put it this way.

> Therefore let no one boast in men. For all things are yours:
> whether Paul or Apollos or Cephas, or the world or life or
> death, or things present or things to come -- all are yours.
> And you *are* Christ's, and Christ *is* God's. (1 Corinthians
> 3:21-23 NKJV).

Because of Jesus Christ these things are now ours.

7. WE ARE NOT PENALIZED FOR SIN

Although the believer experiences physical death, which was the original penalty for sin, we are not penalized in death. Death is the transition to something greater; to be with Christ. The Bible says the following in the Book of Psalms.

> Precious in the sight of the LORD *is* the death of his saints (Psalm 116:15 KJV).

The Holman Christian Standard Bible puts it this way.

> The death of His faithful ones is valuable in the LORD's sight (Psalm 116:15 HCSB)

Death has no victory over believers. In fact, death brings believers directly into His holy presence. Thus, in that sense, death is not to be feared.

Paul emphasized the same thing in his letter to the Corinthians. Death gains no victory over the believers.

> Where, O death, is your victory? Where, O death, is your sting? (1 Corinthians 15:55 NRSV).

The victory of death has been taken away by Jesus Christ. He has been victorious over it. Consequently, the believer in Jesus does not fear death in the same way as the unbeliever.

8. THERE IS A PRESENT POSSESSION OF ETERNAL LIFE FOR THOSE WHO BELIEVE

Jesus told His disciples that those who believe in Him presently have life everlasting.

> Very truly, I tell you, anyone who hears my word and believes him who sent me has eternal life, and does not come under judgment, but has passed from death to life (John 5:24 NRSV).

We have already passed from death unto life. Eternal life is ours right now!

The fact that humans will live forever in the presence of the Lord is a free gift of God. Indeed, we certainly have not earned this. The Bible says.

> For the wages of sin is death, but the free gift of God is eternal life through Christ Jesus our Lord (Romans 6:23 NLT).

Believers are presently experiencing eternal life, an eternal life which will indeed never end!

9. DEATH IS A DEPARTURE TO A NEW DESTINATION

Death, therefore, is a departure to a new destination. We depart from this life to be with Christ. Believers are "at home" with the Lord. Paul wrote.

> Yes, we do have confidence, and we would rather be away from the body and at home with the Lord (2 Corinthians 5:8 NRSV).

Death brings us to a new destination. We are ushered into the presence of the living God. In this sense, death takes us home.

10. BELIEVERS WILL ABIDE FOREVER WITH GOD

The Bible teaches that believers will live forever with the living God. We read of this in the first letter of John. It says.

> The world and its desires pass away, but the man who does the will of God lives forever. . . . See that what you have heard from the beginning remains in you. If it does, you also will remain in the Son and in the Father. And this is what he promised us--even eternal life (1 John 2:17,24-25 NIV).

Our destiny is to be in His presence forever. There will be no end to this relationship between us and Him.

11. WE HAVE A FADELESS INHERITANCE

Scripture speaks of the hope of the believer as being a fadeless inheritance. Peter explained it this way in his first letter. He said.

> Blessed be the God and Father of our Lord Jesus Christ! By his great mercy he has given us a new birth into a living hope through the resurrection of Jesus Christ from the dead, and into an inheritance that is imperishable, undefiled, and unfading, kept in heaven for you, who are being protected by the power of God through faith for a salvation ready to be revealed in the last time (1 Peter 1:3-5 NRSV).

What Jesus Christ has provided for us will never fade away. It will last forever and ever, to the ages of the ages.

12. THERE IS INFINITE VALUE FOR HUMAN BEINGS

Because God has placed such value on human beings in sending His Son to die for our sins, it makes sense that the relationship between the Creator and the created will go beyond this life into eternity. This indeed, is the promise of Scripture.

This briefly sums up some of the things which the New Testament says will happen for those who have died believing in Jesus Christ. These truths are indeed wonderful.

SUMMARY TO QUESTION 16
WHAT HOPE DOES THE NEW TESTAMENT GIVE FOR THE DEAD?

Human beings are all born spiritually dead, separated from the living God. Dying in this state leads to eternal separation from God's presence. This is called the "second death." This is the bad news.

The good news is that humans do not have to be separated from the Lord in this life or in the next. As is true with the Old Testament, the New Testament also provides hope for the living as well as for the dead.

The answers to life and death are all found in the Person of Jesus Christ. Indeed, He has solved the matter of the spiritual separation between God and humanity by His death on Calvary's cross. Jesus took the penalty for sin upon Himself so that we will not have to suffer the consequences. This is the good news, the gospel. All those who trust in Jesus Christ as Savior receive the free gift of eternal life.

From the New Testament we are given further information about the next life. We discover that eternal life begins the moment we trust Jesus Christ as our Savior. Physical death brings the believer immediately into His presence.

However, those who believe in Christ never die in the spiritual sense. In other words, they are never separated from the Lord from the moment they become His child. Once we trust Him as Savior we forever belong to Him.

Death, therefore, is a transition into a better state, a state of being in the presence of God. It is not something for the Christian to ultimately fear.

Consequently death has no authority over the believer because it brings us to another destination; into the everlasting presence of the living God. We move from one destination, earth, to another destination, the presence of the Lord.

We also inherit everything that belongs to Jesus. The treasures of the universe are now ours because we are His children, part of His forever family. This promised inheritance for the believer is eternal. It does not fade.

These are some of the wonderful promises of Scripture. There is indeed hope for the living as well as for the dead.

In What Sense Has
Jesus Abolished Death?

The Bible says that Jesus Christ has abolished, or destroyed, death. Paul wrote the following to Timothy.

> But it has now been revealed through the appearing of our Savior, Christ Jesus, who has destroyed death and has brought life and immortality to light through the gospel (2 Timothy 1:10 NIV).

Since believers still die, in what sense has He accomplished this? How has Jesus destroyed or abolished death?

A number of things need to be observed in answering this question.

JESUS HAS ABOLISHED SPIRITUAL DEATH: PEOPLE DO NOT HAVE TO BE SEPARATED FROM GOD

To begin with, we have to understand what specific death Paul is talking about. The word death in this verse refers to spiritual, not physical, death. By dying on the cross for the sins of the world and rising from the dead, Jesus achieved victory over spiritual death. Humans no longer need to be separated from God in a spiritual sense. We now have life and immortality through Christ. He, therefore, abolished spiritual death in the sense that Christians are made spiritually alive through believing in Him.

Paul wrote to the Romans and explained it in this manner.

> Therefore we have been buried with him by baptism into death, so that, just as Christ was raised from the dead by the glory of the Father, so we too might walk in newness of life. . . So you also must consider yourselves dead to sin and alive to God in Christ Jesus. No longer present your members to sin as instruments of wickedness, but present yourselves to God as those who have been brought from death to life, and present your members to God as instruments of righteousness (Romans 6:4,11,13 NRSV).

We died with Christ and were raised with Him. The penalty for our sins was placed upon Him so that we do not have to suffer for them. The separation or gulf between God and humanity has now been bridged by Jesus Christ.

Thus, spiritual death for the believer has been abolished because of Jesus. We are dead to sin but alive to God through the Person and work of Jesus Christ. No longer will we be separated from God. Jesus' death accomplished this.

JESUS ACHIEVED VICTORY OVER PHYSICAL DEATH

Not only did our Lord abolish spiritual death by His own death on the cross, Jesus Christ has also defeated physical death at His resurrection from the dead. When He came back from the dead, He achieved victory over the powers of death. He said.

> Fear not, I am the first and the last, and the living one. I died, and behold I am alive forevermore, and I have the keys of Death and Hades (Revelation 1:17,18 ESV).

When those who have believed in Christ are resurrected, then the last aspect of death, physical death, will also be abolished.

The Apostle Paul wrote this victorious statement to the Corinthians.

> The last enemy *that* shall be destroyed *is* death (1 Corinthians 15:26 KJV).

This, however, does not mean believers are presently exempt from physical death. What it does mean is that physical death has lost its sting, its power over us.

Paul wrote elsewhere to the Corinthians.

> Death, where is your victory? Death, where is your sting? (1 Corinthians 15:55 God's Word).

Death is a reality, but it does not have the terror it once had because of Jesus. Indeed, death is not the end for the believer or unbeliever. For the believer, we know that something better awaits us; a destination where we will be in the presence of the living God!

ALL DEATH WILL EVENTUALLY BE REMOVED

In God's great plan for time and eternity He has chosen not to remove death, dying and evil all at once. It will not be until the Last Judgment that these things will be no more. At that time they will be once and for all removed. Once He establishes a new heaven and a new earth there will be no more death, dying or pain. We read about this in the Book of Revelation. He said.

> Death and Hades were thrown into the lake of fire. This is the second death, the lake of fire (Revelation 20:14 HCSB).

When speaking of our new life in the Holy City, the New Jerusalem, the Bible describes what we will experience in the following manner.

> He will wipe away every tear from their eyes. Death will exist no longer; grief, crying, and pain will exist no longer, because the previous things have passed away. Then the One seated

on the throne said, "Look! I am making everything new." He also said, "Write, because these words are faithful and true" (Revelation 21:4-5 HCSB).

Death will be done away with! No more pain, crying, tears or dying. What a wonderful future is promised to those who believe!

SUMMARY TO QUESTION 17
IN WHAT SENSE HAS JESUS ABOLISHED DEATH?

Scripture says that Jesus Christ has abolished death. Yet, believers in Christ still die. How then has He abolished death if we still die? How can anyone speak of death as being done away with? In what sense has death been abolished?

The Bible says that Jesus has abolished both physical death and spiritual death through His death on the cross and His resurrection from the dead. The main idea behind death is separation. People are born spiritually separated from God. Jesus Christ made it possible for humankind to become united again with God.

Indeed, His death on the cross of Calvary paid the penalty for our sins. Thus, there does not have to be any spiritual separation ever again between humans and their Creator. Jesus Christ has solved that issue.

Therefore, when a person trusts Jesus Christ as their Savior, they are no longer spiritually dead or spiritually separated from the Lord. Christ has abolished spiritual death for the believer. They are now "in Christ" or united spiritually with Him.

Furthermore, there will never be any more separation between the believer and Christ because spiritual death, or spiritual separation, has been once and for all abolished.

Therefore, those who are only born physically, but not spiritually, will die twice. They will die once physically and they will also die eternally.

Unbelievers will be forever separated from the Lord. This is also known as the "second death."

On the other hand, those who are born twice, once physically and once spiritually, will die only physically. There will be no spiritual death, or separation from God, for those who have trusted Jesus. Instead, they will live eternally with the Lord. Thus, everyone needs that spiritual rebirth.

Jesus Christ has also conquered physical death. Physical death separates the spirit from the body but it does not separate the believer from the Lord. Death is still an enemy but it is only a temporary enemy. The Bible says that all death will eventually be removed.

In His great plan for time and eternity, God has not chosen to remove it all at once. Death is still with us. Yet there will come a day when death will be no more. The Book of Revelation says that death will be thrown into the lake of fire. When this occurs death will no longer exist. Indeed, all things associated with death and dying will be forever destroyed.

This is the glorious future promised in the Word of God. Again, all of this occurs because of the work of Jesus Christ on the cross of Calvary and His resurrection from the dead. He made all these things possible.

QUESTION 18

Who Has The Ultimate Power Over Death: God Or The Devil?

The Bible says that Jesus Christ has authority over life and death. He Himself made this claim. We read about it in the Book of Revelation.

> I am the living one who died. Look, I am alive forever and ever! And I hold the keys of death and the grave (Revelation 1:18 NLT).

According to His own words, Jesus holds the power over death. However the Bible also says that the devil has the power over death. The writer to the Hebrews stated.

> Since the children have flesh and blood, he too shared in their humanity so that by his death he might destroy him who holds the power of death--that is, the devil (Hebrews 2:14,15 NIV).

How can both of these statements be true? Does Christ or the devil have power over death? What is the answer to this question?

DEATH RULED UNTIL CHRIST CAME

Until Christ's coming into the world, death seemed to rule humanity. In this sense, the devil held power over people with the fear of death.

Jesus, we are told, came to destroy the works of the devil. The Apostle John wrote.

> He who sins is of the devil, for the devil has sinned from the beginning. For this purpose the Son of God was manifested, that He might destroy the works of the devil (1 John 3:8 NKJV).

This would include the fear of death that had a hold on people. Once Jesus Christ came and conquered death, the fear was forever gone. Death has no authority over those who have believed in Him.

The writer to the Hebrews put it this way.

> If that had been necessary, he would have had to die again and again, ever since the world began. But no! He came once for all time, at the end of the age, to remove the power of sin forever by his sacrificial death for us (Hebrews 9:26 NLT).

The authority of sin, which includes death, has been removed by the death of Christ. Death has been defeated. This truly is great news!

The Apostle Paul wrote to the Corinthians with this victorious statement. He said.

> For this perishable body must put on the imperishable, and this mortal must put on immortality. Now when this perishable puts on the imperishable, and this mortal puts on immortality, then the saying that is written will happen, "*Death has been swallowed up in victory.*" "*Where, O death, is your victory? Where, O death, is your sting?*" The sting of death is sin, and the power of sin is the law. But thanks be to God, who gives us the victory through our Lord Jesus Christ! So then, dear brothers and sisters, be firm. Do not be moved! Always be outstanding in the work of the Lord, knowing that your labor is not in vain in the Lord (1 Corinthians 15:53-58 NET)

Death cannot ultimately be victorious over the believer. Indeed, the believer has been promised a conscious personal existence in the presence of God after physical death.

Furthermore, there will come a day when the body of the believer will be raised and glorified. This perishable body will be changed to an imperishable one.

Therefore, it is God, and He alone, who has authority over life and death.

SUMMARY TO QUESTION 18
WHO HAS THE ULTIMATE POWER OVER DEATH: GOD OR THE DEVIL?

When sin entered into our world physical death came with it. The author of sin and death is the devil himself. The Bible says that the coming of Jesus Christ into the world was for a number of reasons. One of them was for the purpose of destroying the works of the devil.

Jesus accomplished this by His offering Himself as the sacrifice for sin on Calvary's cross and then coming back from the dead three days later. Since He conquered death those who believe in Him can conquer it also.

Thus, He destroyed the power of death in the sense that death no longer has the fear that it once had. This is true because those who believe in Christ belong to Him forever, and nothing, not even death, can keep the believers and Him apart.

Therefore, the ultimate power of death belongs to Jesus Christ, the one who conquered death and the grave. Indeed, when Paul wrote to the Corinthians, he emphasized that the sting of death has been taken away by Jesus Christ. Jesus Christ has won the victory, death had been defeated.

In the future, there will come a day when death will be entirely done away with. Until that day, we need to look at death as a defeated foe. Jesus Christ has won that victory.

PART 2

Living In The Light Of Eternity

In our first section, we have established the biblical background for conducting our lives in the light of eternity. We have seen that physical death, though it is now a reality, was not God's original intention. Indeed, He created everything perfect. Death came as a result of the sin of Adam and Eve.

Jesus Christ came into the world to be its Savior. His death on the cross made it possible to restore the broken relationship between God and the human race. When a person trusts Christ as their Savior they are spared the second death, eternal death. Indeed, everlasting life in heaven awaits the believer.

However, those who reject Him will spend eternity apart from Christ and His magnificent presence. Consequently, there are only two destinies we as humans face.

Once we understand these foundational truths the Bible gives us about death, dying and the afterlife, then it should affect the way in which we live in this life.

This section considers how to live in light of eternity. How can we live a life that is pleasing to God knowing that eternity awaits us? Can we be certain that we will spend eternity in heaven? If so, then should we be afraid of dying?

What then is the proper response for the death of a loved one who is a believer? Since there will be a final judgment, how do we respond to the death of a loved one who may not have been a believer?

These, as well as other important issues, will be addressed as we consider how we are to live a life that is honoring the Lord in the light of eternity.

QUESTION 19

Can Anyone Be Certain They Are Going To Heaven?

The Bible teaches that there is an eternal God who exists. He is not subject to time. Human beings, on the other hand, are subject to time. Indeed, each of us is limited to a few short years here upon the earth. The Scripture says that after our death, we will spend eternity either with God or without Him.

There is a heaven, there is a hell. Can we be certain that after we die we will go to heaven?

In the state of Indiana there is a tombstone which reads as follows.

> Pause stranger as you pass me by
> As you are now, so once was I
> As I am now, so you will be,
> So prepare for death, and follow me.

One passerby read this thought-provoking message and then scratched the following insightful words.

> To follow you I'm not content,
> Until I know which way you went.

We would like to know exactly where we are going after we die! Can anyone really know? Can we be certain?

The Scripture makes it clear that we can indeed know where we will go after this life is over. We can make the following observations.

1. WE EACH MUST CHOOSE WHOM WE WILL SERVE

Where we will go after our death is determined by our life here upon the earth. In this life, and in this life alone, we must choose whom we will serve. We can either believe the promises of the living God or reject those promises. Choices bring consequences. The choices we make in time will determine where we will spend eternity.

After the nation of Israel had entered the Promised Land, the leader Joshua told the people that they had two basic choices concerning whom they would serve.

> But if serving the LORD seems undesirable to you, then choose for yourselves this day whom you will serve, whether the gods your forefathers served beyond the River, or the gods of the Amorites, in whose land you are living. But as for me and my household, we will serve the LORD (Joshua 24:15 NIV).

Joshua challenged the people to choose whom they would serve. There were these two choices. Would it be the Lord or the non-existent gods of the land of Canaan? Joshua and his household were determined to serve the Lord. In the same manner, each of us must make our own choice as to whether or not we will choose Him.

2. WE CAN KNOW WHERE WE ARE GOING!

The Bible says if we do choose the Lord, then we can know that we will go to heaven when we die. We read this promise in the first letter from John.

> The one who has the Son has life. The one who doesn't have the Son of God does not have life. I have written these things

to you who believe in the name of the Son of God, so that you may know that you have eternal life (1 John 5:12,13 HCSB).

This is a promise of God! We can know that we have everlasting life if we put our faith in Jesus Christ, the Son of God. As we have previously noted, eternal life is something that belongs to believers only. Though unbelievers will exist for eternity, they will not have eternal life. They will be in a state of eternal separation, or eternal death. This is in direct contrast to the future of those who have trusted the God of the Bible.

Furthermore, Scripture says that the Spirit of God testifies to our spirit that we do have eternal life. Paul wrote the following words to the Romans expressing this truth.

> The Spirit Himself testifies together with our spirit that we are God's children (Romans 8:16 HCSB).

We can know that we have life eternal. God's Word promises it and God's Spirit testifies to our spirit that we are His children.

3. CHRISTIANS ALREADY HAVE ETERNAL LIFE

In addition, we discover that the possession of eternal life is something believers presently have. Jesus said it plainly as John records.

> I tell you for certain that everyone who hears my message and has faith in the one who sent me has eternal life and will never be condemned. They have already gone from death to life (John 5:24 CEV).

We have already gone from death to life. Eternal life is ours right now!

4. ETERNAL LIFE IS KNOWING A PERSON

According to the Bible, eternal life is a relationship with a Person, the wonderful Person of Jesus Christ. Jesus Himself testified to this fact.

On the night of His betrayal Jesus prayed the following to God the Father while on His way to the Garden of Gethsemane.

> This is eternal life: that they may know You, the only true God, and the One You have sent —Jesus Christ (John 17:3 HCSB)

Jesus defines eternal life for us. Eternal life begins the moment one enters into a personal relationship with God the Father through God the Son, Jesus Christ. The good news is that it never ends! It is indeed eternal.

5. PAUL KNEW WHOM HE HAD BELIEVED IN

These truths were understood by the New Testament Christians. Paul the Apostle said he knew in whom he had trusted or believed in.

> That is why I am suffering here in prison. But I am not ashamed of it, for I know the one in whom I trust, and I am sure that he is able to guard what I have entrusted to him until the day of his return (2 Timothy 1:12 NLT).

The good news is that we too can know in whom we have believed. Indeed, we can know that we are going to heaven because we can trust the promises the Lord has made to us!

Therefore, from the evidence of the New Testament, we find that eternal life can be ours by trusting Jesus Christ as Savior. Once we believe in Him, we can have the assurance that we are going to heaven. This is what the Bible promises.

SUMMARY TO QUESTION 19
CAN ANYONE BE CERTAIN THEY ARE GOING TO HEAVEN?

Scripture says that heaven is a reality. It also says that we can know for certain that we are going to go to heaven after we die.

The Bible emphasizes that every person must make a choice. They must choose to either believe in the Lord or choose to reject Him. Indeed, there is no middle ground.

The good news of Scripture is that human beings can know that they have eternal life if they believe in Jesus. Trusting Jesus Christ as Savior provides the assurance that life everlasting is ours. We can know where we are going after this life is over. God's Spirit will confirm this truth in our hearts.

Consequently, the Word of God tells us this and the Spirit of God confirms it to us. We do not have to hope that we can make it to heaven; we can know that we are going there!

Furthermore, the Bible says that eternal life is ours right now. Jesus said that those who have believed in Him have already passed from death into life. As soon as we make the decision for Jesus Christ as our Savior, we have eternal life because we have entered into an eternal, personal relationship with Him. This is the promise of God's Word. We also find that the New Testament believers applied this truth to their own lives. The Apostle Paul emphasized that he knew in whom he had believed. We too can know also in whom we have believed if we trust what the Word of God says.

Can we know we are going to heaven? Absolutely!

How Do Non-Christians Face Death?

Those who do not believe that the Bible is God's Word still have to deal with the problem of death. They too must face the great unknown. It is something that nobody looks forward to facing. The humorist Woody Allen said.

> I don't mind dying. I just don't want to be there when it happens.

That sentiment sums up of the feeling of a lot of people.

THE TERRIFYING NATURE OF DEATH

The Bible recognizes that all of us have a natural fear of death. In fact, in the Book Job it is called the "king of terrors."

> He is torn from the security of his tent and marched off to the king of terrors (Job 18:14 NIV).

This is an apt description of death.

The psalmist also recognized the terrifying nature of death. He spoke of the anguish of death when he wrote the following.

> My heart is in anguish within me, the terrors of death have fallen upon me (Psalm 55:4 NRSV).

The fear of death can be a terrifying thing.

The writer to the Hebrews said those who fear death are actually in bondage to a type of slavery. He put it this way.

> And free those who all their lives were held in slavery by the fear of death (Hebrews 2:15 NRSV).

Those who are afraid of death are indeed enslaved.

SOME NON-CHRISTIAN APPROACHES TO DEATH

Non-believers deal with death in a variety of ways. The following are some of the approaches or attitudes in which they face the issue of the afterlife.

APPROACH 1: THEY NEVER WANT TO THINK ABOUT DEATH

Among many people there is often the unwillingness to face the fact that their death is inevitable. Indeed, it is something they never try to think about. Our modern world has helped with this attitude.

For example, we no longer use the term graveyards but rather they are called memorial parks. People speak of a person "passing away" or "expiring." They are almost afraid to use the word "death." When a person does die the mortician does everything that he or she can to hide the fact that that person has died. The dead are made to look so natural. Consequently, death is never a topic that many everyday people think about or even prepare for. In other words, it happens to someone else, not to them.

RESPONSE

Try as they might not to think about it, death will come to everyone. When reality does hit, it is usually followed by sheer terror. Since the unbeliever has not prepared for their own death they are usually numb when they discover that their death may be imminent.

APPROACH 2: THERE IS THE DENIAL OF DEATH

Some people deny the reality of death. In other words, they think death is just an illusion. Therefore, they claim they have nothing to fear since death does not really occur. There are a number of religions as well as other systems of belief that actually hold this view. Death, to them, is not real.

RESPONSE

Unfortunately no one can live consistently with this idea. It is a denial of the obvious. Death is a reality we all must face. Pretending it does not exist will not make it go away. Those who deny that death exists eventually experience what they say does not happen. They die.

APPROACH 3: SOME SAY WE CANNOT KNOW WHAT WILL HAPPEN

Many people think that it is impossible to know what will happen to people after this life. Consequently death is something that is out of the realm of discussion. They live their life as an agnostic toward death. This is one who does not know, and believes they cannot know, what will happen in the future. Therefore, the issue is not discussed.

RESPONSE

By taking this position, they have shut themselves off from biblical revelation; the only place where humans can go to receive an answer as to what will happen after this life is over.

In other words, they have ruled out ahead of time the possibility of discovering answers without even checking out any possible answers!

APPROACH 4: MANY THINK THAT DEATH IS THE END

According to many people, there is no hereafter. Death is the end of all existence. Life developed on this planet by the chance forces of mind-less evolution. Everything, including humanity, is a result of natural forces. Since there is no supernatural, there is nothing that happens to a human being after death. The material that makes up the human body will eventually dissolve. Nothing will be left of that person.

Paul wrote of people like this. He said.

> There is no fear of God before their eyes (Romans 3:18 KJV).

The New Living Translation puts it this way.

> They have no fear of God to restrain them (Romans 3:18 NLT).

These people live without any respect toward the Lord because they think death is the end of everything. We are born, we live, and then we die. That's it.

RESPONSE

Yet the Bible says humans are made for eternity. Death is not the end. Scripture not only makes the claim, it provides evidence to back it up. Indeed, there are plenty of reasons to believe that this life is not all that there is. Indeed, the evidence shows that we have been made for all eternity.

APPROACH 5: SOME ARE FATALISTIC TOWARD DEATH

Fatalism sees everything in life as pre-ordained. What will be, will be. We really can't do anything about anything. This includes death. Since humanity does not have any say in the matter, each person should be unconcerned about death.

RESPONSE

The Bible teaches that it is our decision as to where we will spend eternity, not the decision of fate. We are held personally responsible for the decisions we make. Jesus said.

That is why I said you will die with your sins unforgiven. If you don't have faith in me for who I am, you will die, and your sins will not be forgiven" (John 8:24 CEV).

It is our choice where we will spend eternity. Our destiny has not been predetermined before our birth.

APPROACH 6: THERE IS A FALSE OPTIMISM ON BEHALF OF SOME

Some have a false optimism toward death. They believe that everything will be fine in the next life. Perhaps they have heard stories of people who have had stopped breathing for a short period of time and then have been resuscitated. Some of these people testify that their time on "the other side" showed them that everything is great. They say that there is nothing to be afraid of. Death is not to be feared.

RESPONSE

This hope is based upon a false optimism. Scripture gives no such hope to all who have died. The Bible says.

> There is no peace, says my God, for the wicked (Isaiah 57:21 NRSV).

If a person has not made peace with God in this life, there is no hope for them in the next. Death cuts off that person from the possibility of obtaining eternal life.

APPROACH 7: SOME BECOME RELIGIOUS MARTYRS

Many people have died for some religious cause thinking that it will usher them into some type of heavenly existence. Their religion teaches them that the afterlife can be gained by dying a martyr's death. Consequently death takes on the idea of promotion to something better.

RESPONSE

Unfortunately, there is no objective basis for their belief. Dying for a cause will not automatically bring one into heaven, no matter how noble the cause. Faith is only as good as the object in which it is placed. Faith in a misguided object will not bring anyone into heaven. Heaven will only be achieved by putting ones faith in Jesus Christ.

APPROACH 8: THERE IS ALSO AN ESCAPIST ATTITUDE

For many, death is something they do not want to ever think about. Consequently they live life as an escapist. Escapism can take many forms: work, money, alcohol, drugs, school, or pleasure. Whatever form of escape people take, it is in an effort not to think about the hereafter. By devoting themselves to other pursuits, they have busied themselves to the place where they do not have to think about the afterlife.

RESPONSE

The Bible warns about those who attempt to escape the responsibilities of dealing with God by turning to money or power. Jesus said.

> Then he said, "Beware! Don't be greedy for what you don't have. Real life is not measured by how much we own" (Luke 12:15 NLT).

There is no escaping the judgment of God. No amount of diversion will change this fact.

APPROACH 9: SOME LOSE ALL HOPE

Finally, there are those who lose all hope and eventually take their own life. They think this will end their trouble. Death, to them, is the ultimate escape to all their problems.

RESPONSE

Death is not the end. By taking their own life they have not solved the problem. They still have to face the judgment of God. The writer to the Hebrews said.

And just as it is destined that each person dies only once and after that comes judgment (Hebrews 9:27 NLT).

A person who takes their own life will not solve any problem by this act. Death is not the end. Indeed, it merely leads to another destination.

This sums up some of the responses which non-Christians give to the death problem. These responses, however, do not answer anything.

SUMMARY TO QUESTION 20
HOW DO NON-CHRISTIANS FACE DEATH?

If the Bible had nothing to say about the afterlife, then we would have no hope whatsoever. Fortunately we do not have to be in the dark with respect to the next world because the living God has spoken. We do have answers!

Non-Christians, like Christians, have to face the inevitability of death. They deal with the issue in various ways. Some of the more popular ways include the following.

To begin with, many people ignore the topic of death. Intellectually they know that they will someday die but they never think about it or prepare for it. Death is what happens to someone else, not to them. However, when they realize that death will soon visit them they are usually terrified since they have lived their entire life without ever giving the subject a second thought. Panic usually sets in at this time.

There are those who deny that death is a reality. Death, according to some, does not really exist. It is an illusion. Of course, denying the reality of death does not stop that person from dying.

Others say no one can really know what happens after death so they don't bother with the issue. They do not believe that anyone does know the answer, or even can know. So the question is avoided.

However, avoidance of the question will not make it go away. Furthermore, the Bible says there is an answer and that we can know that answer.

Many take the stance that death is the end of all existence. Consequently, we must live this life to the fullest because this is all that there is. Yet, the Bible says that there is something all of us will have to face after death; a God who will judge us.

It is also popular to have a fatalistic view toward death. To some individuals, everything has been predetermined by some force so that nobody can do anything about death or dying. It will happen the way it is meant to happen. On the other hand, the Bible says that we have choice. We can choose to believe or not to believe. Whatever choice we make will determine where we spend eternity. It is up to us.

Some have a false optimism assuming everything will be fine. They have come to believe that death is actually a doorway to a better life for all of us. Yet, these people reject the clear teaching of Scripture that everything will not be fine for countless people. Indeed, those who reject Jesus will have to spend eternity apart from Him in a terrible place of punishment.

In some religions, people become martyrs. They assume this will help them gain a better standing in the next world. The trouble with this view is that there is no evidence to support it. The mere fact that someone is sincere, or that they die believing that they are going to a better place, does not make it so. Faith is only as good as the object in which it is placed and Scripture says dying the death of a martyr makes no difference whatsoever as to whether or not a person will enter heaven. The only way to heaven is belief in Jesus.

There are also the escapists who try to avoid thinking about the problem. They often use various substances to numb themselves to the idea of death and dying. However, attempting to escape from the problem of death and dying will not make it go away. Eventually they will have to face the reality of death.

Finally, there are those who lose all hope and take their own life. Most of them suppose that will be the end. Yet the Bible says it is not. Each of us has an appointment with God. Judgment is coming for the unbeliever.

As we have seen, none of these responses to death have any basis in reality. They are merely forms of denial of the biblical truth about this life and the next. The question of death and its inevitability must be faced. The good news is that there are answers to our questions about the afterlife. These answers are found in God's Word, the Bible.

Should Christians Be Afraid Of Dying?

Scripture says that this life is not all that there is. Indeed, we are beings which have been made for eternity. Death is the doorway to eternity for each of us. This eternity will be one of a conscious existence.

Consequently, a person must be prepared. So we ask the obvious question, "How then should the believer in Jesus Christ view their own death?" Should we be afraid of dying? To answer this question we can make the following observations.

THERE IS A NATURAL FEAR OF DEATH

To begin with, we must appreciate the fact that all of us have a natural fear of death. Death is an unknown for each of us. Indeed, we have never been dead before!

In addition, eternity is a long time. These factors will naturally cause an uneasiness or fear of death. This is normal.

In fact, there are examples of godly biblical characters which feared death. We read the following account of King Hezekiah.

> In those days Hezekiah became ill and was at the point of death. The prophet Isaiah son of Amoz went to him and said, "This is what the LORD says: Put your house in order, because you are going to die; you will not recover." Hezekiah

turned his face to the wall and prayed to the LORD, "Remember, O LORD, how I have walked before you faithfully and with wholehearted devotion and have done what is good in your eyes." And Hezekiah wept bitterly (2 Kings 20:1-3 NIV).

Hezekiah, a godly king, was afraid of dying. Therefore, we should not think it strange if we have the same type of fear.

DEATH SHOULD NOT ULTIMATELY BE FEARED BY THE BELIEVER

While believers do have a natural fear of death there should be no ultimate fear. Although the believer has to suffer physical death because of the original sin of Adam, death loses its horror because it transports the believer into a better life.

Therefore, once we understand what happens to us at death, it is not something to be feared. Though it is the separation of the spirit and the body, it is a separation into something better.

In fact, the Bible says that Jesus came to release us from the fear of death and dying. We read the following in the letter to the Hebrews.

Because God's children are human beings-- made of flesh and blood-- Jesus also became flesh and blood by being born in human form. For only as a human being could he die, and only by dying could he break the power of the Devil, who had the power of death. Only in this way could he deliver those who have lived all their lives as slaves to the fear of dying (Hebrews 2:14-15 NLT).

Notice that it says that Jesus delivers us from the fear of dying.

How then should we look at death? For the believer a number of factors need to be considered. They can be summed up as follows.

1. DEATH IS NOT THE END

Death is a transition, it is not an end. Consequently the ultimate terror of death is removed for those who trust in the promises of the God of Scripture. David wrote.

> I may walk through valleys as dark as death, but I won't be afraid. You are with me, and your shepherd's rod makes me feel safe (Psalm 23:4 CEV).

From the Word of God, we are told that believers can know that the Lord is with them when they have to face death. In one sense, they only enter the valley of the shadow of death, not the reality.

Why is this so? Although believers do die physically, there is not the same separation as the unbeliever experiences in death. This is because physical death brings us immediately into the presence of the Lord. Therefore, not even death can separate the believer from the Lord.

2. DEATH IS A SOURCE OF BLESSING FOR THE BELIEVER

The Bible teaches that death is a source of blessing to the believer in Jesus Christ. The psalmist proclaimed this truth.

> Precious in the sight of the LORD is the death of his saints (Psalm 116:15 NIV).

It is precious because we go to be with Him. Indeed, there is no longer any separation between us.

In addition, the Apostle Paul wrote of the desire of each of us to have our bodies redeemed or changed. He said the following to the Romans.

> And even we Christians, although we have the Holy Spirit within us as a foretaste of future glory, also groan to be released from pain and suffering. We, too, wait anxiously for that day when God will give us our full rights as his children,

including the new bodies he has promised us (Romans 8:23 NLT).

Those who know Jesus Christ are longing to be with Him. Death will be a blessing for those of us who have trusted Him. Among other things we will be given new bodies, perfect ones.

3. THERE IS A PLACE WHICH IS BEING PREPARED FOR BELIEVERS

The Bible says that a place is now being prepared for believers. On the night of His betrayal, Jesus gave the following words of comfort to His disciples.

> Let not your hearts be troubled. Believe in God; believe also in me. In my Father's house are many rooms. If it were not so, would I have told you that I go to prepare a place for you? And if I go and prepare a place for you, I will come again and will take you to myself, that where I am you may be also (John 14:1-3 ESV).

There is a place that Jesus is preparing for believers. It is called "the Father's House." Thus, we are being prepared a special place in the house of a loving Father.

4. THE CITIZENSHIP OF BELIEVERS IS IN HEAVEN

Christians have their ultimate citizenship in heaven. When Paul wrote to the church at Philippi he emphasized this truth.

> But our citizenship is in heaven, and from it we await a Savior, the Lord Jesus Christ, who will transform our lowly body to be like his glorious body, by the power that enables him even to subject all things to himself (Philippians 3:20,21 ESV).

The believer is a citizen of two worlds. Although we live here upon the earth our true home is with God in heaven. The Bible says we are merely temporary residents, or pilgrims, here upon the earth.

In fact, Peter addressed his first letter to these pilgrims. He wrote the following to the Christians.

> Peter, an apostle of Jesus Christ, To the pilgrims of the Dispersion in Pontus, Galatia, Cappadocia, Asia, and Bithynia (1 Peter 1:1 NKJV)

The New English Translation puts it this way.

> From Peter, an apostle of Jesus Christ, to those temporarily residing abroad (in Pontus, Galatia, Cappadocia, the province of Asia, and Bithynia) who are chosen (1 Peter 1:1 NET).

Our real home is in heaven, not upon this earth. We are only temporarily residing here.

5. WE HAVE A GENUINE HOPE FOR SOMETHING SO MUCH BETTER

Consequently, we have a realistic hope for an existence that will be so much better in the next life. Therefore, the Bible tells us not to sorrow for the dead believers as unbelievers sorrow for their dead. Paul wrote to the Thessalonians and made this clear. He said.

> And now, brothers and sisters, I want you to know what will happen to the Christians who have died so you will not be full of sorrow like people who have no hope (1 Thessalonians 4:13 NLT).

Notice the contrast. Believers have a genuine hope. Death is not the end. Therefore, any sorrow we may express for believers who have died is always mixed with the feeling of happiness for them. They have gone on to glory. This is in contrast to those who have died outside of Christ who have no hope of eternal life in the presence of the Lord.

LIVING IN THE LIGHT OF ETERNITY

6. DEATH IS NOT A PUNISHMENT FOR BELIEVERS

While those who believe in Jesus Christ, like non-believers, will suffer physical death, it must be emphasized that death is not a punishment for those who have trusted Christ. The Bible says that there is no condemnation for those who have believed in Jesus. Paul wrote.

> Therefore, there is now no condemnation for those who are
> in Christ Jesus (Romans 8:1 NIV).

Jesus Christ has paid the penalty for all of our sins on the cross of Calvary. In fact, we do not pay for any of them! Therefore, we should not see our death as some sort of punishment from God.

Indeed, it is not. Death has been passed on to the entire human race because of the original sin of Adam and Eve. As we have emphasized, we die because we were born into a fallen world which results in the eventual death of every person.

While this world remains in a fallen or imperfect state, people will continue to die. Just as Christians experience all of the evils associated with our fallen world, so too we will experience sickness and eventually physical death.

Yet death for the believer is not a personal judgment against us. In fact, it is a promotion! When believers die we enter into the presence of the Lord. In His presence we will be rewarded, not condemned! Therefore, we move into something infinitely better!

7. THERE IS NO COMPARISON BETWEEN THIS LIFE AND THE NEXT

Realizing all these things should help us put this life into proper perspective. The Apostle Paul said there is no real comparison between this life and the blessings of the next.

Paul made this clear when he wrote to the Romans. He said the following.

> For I consider that the sufferings of this present time are not
> worth comparing with the glory that is to be revealed to us
> (Romans 8:18 ESV).

Friends and riches will be far greater in heaven than what is here upon
the earth. In fact, everything worthwhile will be greater in heaven.
Therefore, death is victory for the believer.

The Apostle Paul also wrote these words of triumph to the believers in
Corinth.

> O Death, where is your victory? O Death, where is your
> sting? Now the sting of death is sin, and the power of sin
> is the law. But thanks be to God, who gives us the victory
> through our Lord Jesus Christ! (1 Corinthians 15:55-57
> HCSB).

The victory over death has been won through Jesus Christ. Ultimately,
there is nothing to fear.

All of these things should be taken into consideration when we think
about our own death. Indeed, it is an eternal promotion into God's
wonderful presence!

SUMMARY TO QUESTION 21
SHOULD CHRISTIANS BE AFRAID OF DYING?

As human beings, we all have a normal fear of death. While a certain
anxiety about the afterlife is natural, believers in Jesus Christ should
not be obsessed with the idea of death and dying. Neither should we let
the fear of death keep us from being effective here on the earth. There
are a number of reasons as to why this is so.

Death is not something to be ultimately feared by the believer in
Christ. Among other things, Jesus Christ came to earth for the purpose
of removing the fear of death. According to Scripture, death is merely

the process of moving from one sphere of existence to the next. It is not the end. Indeed, it is not moving from existence to non-existence.

The Lord Jesus said that He is presently preparing a place for every believer in the house of His Father. Each of us who know Jesus Christ as our Savior has a home in heaven, a home with a gracious loving Father. This is indeed a comforting thought.

Furthermore, the Bible says that our citizenship is in heaven. This is where we ultimately belong. Since the citizenship of the believer is not of this world, the departure from this world is something that will be joyous. We will move into our real home.

Indeed, we are called temporary residents and pilgrims in this world. We are merely passing through this life.

Something else needs to be emphasized about death. We all have to die physically because we still live in a fallen world, an imperfect world. The original sin of Adam and Eve brought physical death to all of us. Thus, death is the natural result of living in this world but it is not a personal judgment against us for our individual sin.

Indeed, death is never seen in the New Testament as a punishment for believers. Death is a promotion. Jesus took the punishment of our sin upon Himself. He was punished so we do not have to be punished. Consequently, we do not have to look at our death as a punishment.

Finally, Scripture emphasizes there is no comparison of this life to the next. Indeed, everything will be greater in heaven. Anything we have in this life is nothing compared to what awaits us in the next.

We should keep all of these things in mind when contemplating our own death. If we do, then death will hold no ultimate fear for the believer.

QUESTION 22

Are Life And Death Under God's Control?

Unless a person takes their own life, death does not occur at a time of our own choosing. In fact, it usually happens when we least expect it. Though death is an experience that is not in our control, it is not out of the control of the God of the Bible. Scripture has the following to say about the subject.

LIFE AND DEATH ARE UNDER GOD'S CONTROL

The Bible says that life and death, and everything else for that matter, are under the control of the God of Scripture. This is illustrated so many times in Holy Scripture.

EXAMPLE 1: THE TWO WITNESSES IN THE BOOK OF REVELATION WILL BE KEPT FROM DYING

For example, we read the Lord saying the following in the Book of Revelation about two witnesses which will come to the earth at some time in the future.

> And I will give power to my two witnesses, and they will prophesy for 1,260 days, clothed in sackcloth. These are the two olive trees and the two lampstands that stand before the Lord of the earth. If anyone tries to harm them, fire comes from their mouths and devours their enemies. This

is how anyone who wants to harm them must die. These men have power to shut up the sky so that it will not rain during the time they are prophesying; and they have power to turn the waters into blood and to strike the earth with every kind of plague as often as they want. Now when they have finished their testimony, the beast that comes up from the Abyss will attack them, and overpower and kill them (Revelation 11:3-7 NIV).

Notice that these two people were not allowed to die until their testimony was finished. Even though their enemies wished to harm them, they were not able. It is not until their testimony is finished that they are able to die.

In the same manner, each of us has a testimony to finish. Like the two witnesses, we will die only when our testimony is finished. This is because the God of the Bible controls life and death.

The psalmist recognized this. He said.

Our God is a God who saves; from the Sovereign LORD comes escape from death (Psalm 68:20 NIV).

The Lord allows His people to escape death when their time on earth is not finished. Again, life and death are completely under His control.

The psalmist also realized that his time on earth was in the hand of the Lord. He made the following declaration of this.

My times are in your hand; deliver me from the hand of my enemies and persecutors (Psalm 31:15 NRSV).

Our times are truly in God's hand.

Therefore, Scripture is clear; our lives are under the control of the God of the Bible. He is the Lord of the universe and hence all things are under His power.

EXAMPLE 2: THE LORD WILL NOT ALLOW CERTAIN UNBELIEVERS TO DIE

Not only do we find the Lord protecting the two witnesses from death during the Great Tribulation period, we also discover that during this time the Lord will not permit those being punished to die. We read the following about what will happen to these unbelievers.

> In those days people will seek death, but will not be able to find it; they will long to die, but death will flee from them (Revelation 9:6 NET)

This is a further indication that life and death are completely under His control. Thus, the Lord will not only protect the two witnesses, He will also supernaturally keep the unbelievers from dying for a period of time.

EXAMPLE 3: GOD ALLOWED HEZEKIAH TO LIVE AN EXTRA FIFTEEN YEARS

We have another illustration of this truth. This is from the Old Testament. God told King Hezekiah of Judah that he was going to die. He prayed that the Lord would let him live longer. God granted his request. The Lord gave the following command to the prophet Isaiah.

> "Go and say to Hezekiah, Thus says the Lord, the God of David your father: I have heard your prayer; I have seen your tears. Behold, I will add fifteen years to your life (Isaiah 38:5 ESV).

The good king was granted fifteen extra years. This further shows that life and death are ultimately under God's control.

EXAMPLE 4: DANIEL TOLD BELSHAZZAR THAT GOD HOLDS OUR VERY BREATH IN HIS HAND

This truth is vividly stated in an episode with the prophet Daniel; the famous incident of the handwriting on the wall. Daniel, when called to read the handwriting on the wall in the city of Babylon told the

Babylonian King Belshazzar that God holds our very life and breath in His hand. Daniel spoke these words to the king.

> You have exalted yourself against the Lord of heaven! The vessels of his temple have been brought in before you, and you and your lords, your wives and your concubines have been drinking wine from them. You have praised the gods of silver and gold, of bronze, iron, wood, and stone, which do not see or hear or know; but the God in whose power is your very breath, and to whom belong all your ways, you have not honored (Daniel 5:23 NRSV).

Our ability to breathe is determined by the Lord. Everything in the universe runs at His pleasure. This includes our very breath.

These four biblical examples are highly instructive. Without a doubt, the Scripture teaches that God is in control of our life and our death. Everything is indeed in His hands.

SUMMARY TO QUESTION 22
ARE LIFE AND DEATH UNDER GOD'S CONTROL?

Death is an enemy to humanity, but it is certainly not out of God's control. The Bible says that the God of Scripture controls life and death as well as everything else. Indeed, all things in this universe are subject to His power.

Scripture says that God ordains the number of days that we will live on this earth. He has the power to shorten or prolong each human life. It is His choice alone. There are a number of examples of this in Scripture. We cited four of them.

First, in the Book of Revelation we find that two witnesses, whom the Lord will send to earth, will be granted to live and minister for a specific amount of time. Indeed, they will remain alive until He is finished with them. While others will try to kill them, they will not be able to do it. It will only be when the Lord allows them to die that they will die. Their time, like our time, is in the hand of God.

In another example, there will be unbelievers during the time of the Great Tribulation that will actually seek death but God will not allow them to die! Therefore, during this future time, we have an example of the Lord supernaturally protecting the two witnesses from death as well as supernaturally not allowing the unbelievers to die.

Next, we also find that God extended the life of the good King Hezekiah for fifteen years after He told the king that he was about to die. In prayer, Hezekiah asked to live longer and God granted His request. God alone has that power.

Finally, according to Daniel the prophet, God holds our very breath in His hand. We breathe at His pleasure. During the famous episode of the handwriting on the wall, Daniel told the pagan King Belshazzar that his ability to breathe was controlled by the God of Abraham, Isaac, and Jacob. This is the God whom this pagan king insulted! Belshazzar paid for that sin with his life.

These examples make it clear that the Lord is in control of all aspects of our living and of our dying. In other words, God is in complete control of all things. For those of us who know Him, this is truly a comforting thought.

QUESTION 23

Is There An Appointed Time Each Of Us Must Die?

The Bible makes it clear that life, death, and everything else in the universe is under the control of the God of the Bible. Since life and death are under His control this brings up the question of the timing of our own death. Is there an appointed time in which we must die? Has this been determined for us, or do we have any say in this matter? Christians are divided on this important question. We will look at what each side has to say.

THE CASE FOR AN APPOINTED TIME FOR EACH OF US TO DIE

Those who believe that God has an appointed time for each of us to die usually point to the following passages to substantiate their case.

1. THE STATEMENTS IN JOB ABOUT DYING

In the Book of Job we read that God has set appointed times when people will die. The suffering patriarch Job said.

> You have decided the length of our lives. You know how many months we will live, and we are not given a minute longer (Job 14:5 NLT).

This statement is clear; we will not live one minute longer than we are supposed to live. God has determined this.

2. THE STATEMENTS ABOUT LIFE AND DEATH IN DEUTERONOMY

In another place, the Lord said that He is the One who puts people to death and makes others alive. We read the following words of the Lord in Deuteronomy.

> See now that I myself am He! There is no god besides me. I put to death and I bring to life, I have wounded and I will heal, and no one can deliver out of my hand (Deuteronomy 32:39 NIV)

This verse shows that the Lord Himself controls life and death. Everything! He determines when we live as well as having the control over when we will die.

3. THE WORDS OF PAUL IN ATHENS

The Apostle Paul proclaimed God's control of life and death. In the city of Athens he told a crowd of people that the God of the Bible gives life and breath to all humans. He put it this way to this skeptical crowd.

> Nor is he served by human hands, as though he needed anything, since he himself gives to all mortals life and breath and all things. From one ancestor he made all nations to inhabit the whole earth, and he allotted the times of their existence and the boundaries of the places where they would live (Acts 17:25,26 NRSV).

It is interesting that Paul stated that God allots the times of our existence. In other words, nations, as well as individual people, are subject to His will.

4. THE WORDS OF THE PSALMIST

The psalmist wrote about our lives having been laid out ahead of time by the Lord. Indeed, he made this very plain by his words. He said.

You saw me before I was born. Every day of my life was recorded in your book. Every moment was laid out before a single day had passed (Psalm 139:16 NLT).

There is a time to live and a time to die. Consequently, God has all of our days numbered and we will not live one day longer than He has chosen.

THE CASE THAT THERE IS NOT AN APPOINTED TIME EACH OF US MUST DIE

Not every believer thinks the Bible teaches that each of us has an appointed time in which we must die. While recognizing that God is in control of all things, they do not think the case for an appointed time is actually taught in Scripture.

THE REFERENCE IN THE BOOK OF JOB IS NOT DECISIVE

While the reference in Job 14 seems to solve the issue, it is not that decisive. While it is true that Job 14:5 says that we cannot live one minute longer than God has decided, this is not necessarily God's Word on this issue. The speeches in Job, including this one, contain truth mixed with error. After these speeches were given by Job and his friends the Lord interrupted what was taking place. We read.

Then the LORD answered Job from the whirlwind: "Who is this that questions my wisdom with such ignorant words?" (Job 38:1-2 NIV).

Since the Lord called the previous discussions "ignorant words," we need to be careful about drawing biblical truth from what was said.

THE OTHER PASSAGES ARE NOT DECISIVE EITHER

In addition, the other passages used to support this view do not really say what some people believe that they say. In point of fact, there is nothing directly stated by the Lord Himself, or by one of His prophets, that He has predetermined the exact moment of our death.

Indeed, while we are told that God allows the amount of time we will live and that He has our very breath in His hand, it does not necessarily mean that He determines when the time of our death will occur. All it is saying is that He is control of all things.

In fact, knowing the time of our death is not the same as predetermining it. To what extent He predetermines everything that takes place in our lives is debated among Bible-believers.

Whatever the answer may be, all agree that the God of the Bible is certainly in control of all things including life and death.

What we also know for certain is that the time of our death, though known to God, is unknown to us. Therefore, we must live each day with the realization that it may be our last.

SUMMARY TO QUESTION 23
IS THERE AN APPOINTED TIME EACH OF US MUST DIE?

The God of the Bible is in absolute control of our destinies. All Bible-believers recognize this. This is not a real issue. Does this mean that He has predetermined the exact moment when we will die? Is there a plan which has already been worked out? What does the Bible have to say?

Bible-believing Christians are divided on this issue. There are passages which seem to teach that God does ordain every step we take and that He has pre-determined the exact number of minutes we will live. Before we are born, every moment of our life has been ordered or determined by God. Many people believe this is the case.

On the other hand, these passages which speak of God's control do not have to be understood in this manner. God can still be in complete control of all things while also giving us the ability to make legitimate choices for ourselves.

In sum, God's sovereignty or control does not necessitate that He controls or predetermines every detail of our life. While this may be the case, it is not necessarily. Knowing what will happen to us is not the same as predetermining what will happen.

What we do know is this: God is in complete control of our life and death and He knows when and where we are going to die.

Since *we* do not know when death will occur, we should not let this be a distraction to us. Our job is to live a life which is pleasing to Him and be ready to meet our Maker at any time.

Can We Lengthen Or Shorten Our Life By Our Own Behavior?

Although the Bible says that life and death are ultimately in the hands of God, our behavior can actually affect the length of our lives here upon the earth. In other words, it matters how we behave. We can make the following observations from Scripture.

THERE ARE BIBLICAL PRINCIPLES FOR A LONG LIFE

To begin with, Scripture gives principles that can allow us to live a long life upon the earth. However, God does not guarantee that someone will live long if they follow these principles. Other factors can come in to play. Still, the Bible does say the following.

> The fear of the LORD adds length to life, but the years of the wicked are cut short (Proverbs 10:27 NIV).

The Lord can lengthen the life of those who know Him. On the other hand, the years of the unrighteous can be shortened.

As Israel was about to enter the Promised Land, Moses told the people of that nation that keeping the commandments of the Lord would contribute to them living a long life. This long life would also be a prosperous one. He wrote.

> Keep his decrees and commands, which I am giving you today, so that it may go well with you and your children after

you and that you may live long in the land the LORD your
God gives you for all time (Deuteronomy 4:40 NIV).

Long and prosperous would be the result of the lives of those who kept
the commandments of the Lord. On the other hand, ignoring God's
commands could lead to a shortened life and certainly not a prosperous one.

The New Testament echoes this truth. When the Apostle Paul wrote
to the Ephesians he cited one of the Ten Commandments. It gives the
following promise.

> Obey your father and your mother, and you will have a long
> and happy life (Ephesians 6:2-3 CEV).

These are important principles that the Lord has set down. Obedience to
the Lord by keeping His commandments will lead to a prosperous life.

THERE WERE CERTAIN PEOPLE WHO DIED PREMATURELY

Disobeying the commands of the Lord caused some people to die a
premature death. In fact, the Scripture records the accounts of certain
people who died prematurely as a result of their sin.

1. SAUL DIED EARLY BECAUSE OF SIN

In the Old Testament, we are told that King Saul's life was cut short
because of his unfaithfulness to the commandments of the Lord.

As the King of Israel, he was responsible to be an example of faithful-
ness. He was not. We read about his judgment in Chronicles.

> Saul died because he was unfaithful to the LORD; he did not
> keep the word of the LORD and even consulted a medium
> for guidance, and did not inquire of the LORD. So the
> LORD put him to death and turned the kingdom over to
> David son of Jesse (1 Chronicles 10:13-14 NIV).

Here is a specific example of a person dying because of his unfaithfulness to the Lord. Turning his back on the Lord, this king sought a medium, a spiritist, for guidance. His sinful behavior cost him his life.

2. SOME BELIEVERS IN THE CITY OF CORINTH DIED EARLY

The New Testament emphasizes the same thing. Sinful conduct can actually shorten the lives of believers. The Bible speaks of certain people dying prematurely because of some sin in their life. One illustration of this is found in the letter to the Corinthians.

The Apostle Paul said some of the believers at the church in Corinth died prematurely because of abuses at the Lord's Supper.

He explained it in this manner.

> For if you eat the bread or drink the cup without honoring the body of Christ, you are eating and drinking God's judgment upon yourself. That is why many of you are weak and sick and some have even died. But if we would examine ourselves, we would not be judged by God in this way. Yet when we are judged by the Lord, we are being disciplined so that we will not be condemned along with the world (1 Corinthians 11:29-32 NLT).

These believers died prematurely because of sin. In particular, it was not properly observing the Lord's Supper. Instead of honoring the death of the Lord Jesus they were turning it into a public mockery. This mockery cost them their lives.

3. ANANIAS AND SAPPHIRA WERE JUDGED TO DEATH

In the Book of Acts, we are told of two believers, Ananias and Sapphira, who died prematurely because they lied to God about the price of some parcel of land that they had sold (Acts 5:1-11). Their death shocked the Christians. Indeed, the Bible says that fear fell upon believers after this event. We read in the Book of Acts.

And great fear came upon the whole church and upon all who heard of these things (Acts 5:11 ESV).

The New Testament says that these two people were judged for lying to God. They had a choice and they chose to lie. The Bible tells us that they paid the penalty for lying with their lives. This set an example for the early church and it should set one for us. We should not trifle with the Lord.

THEY WERE JUDGED TO PHYSICAL DEATH, NOT ETERNAL DEATH

In the examples of the New Testament believers it must be emphasized that these Christians experienced physical death, not eternal separation from God. Their physical death did not cost them their eternal soul.

The Apostle Paul wrote about one such person who was being judged. He put it this way.

> In the name of our Lord Jesus Christ, when you are gathered together, along with my spirit, with the power of our Lord Jesus Christ, deliver such a one to Satan for the destruction of the flesh, that his spirit may be saved in the day of the Lord Jesus (1 Corinthians 5:4,5 NKJV).

This man's sinful nature, or life, was to be destroyed if he did not repent. He would die. However, his spirit would be saved at the time of the Lord's judgment. This is the consistent teaching of Scripture; the believer is secure in Jesus Christ.

Therefore, we learn that obedience to the Lord can lead to a long life here upon the earth, while disobedience, particularly of a public nature, can lead to premature death. Knowing this truth should cause us to be careful about what we do and what we say.

SUMMARY TO QUESTION 24
CAN WE LENGTHEN OR SHORTEN OUR LIFE BY OUR BEHAVIOR?

The Bible makes it clear that God is in control of everything. This includes how long we will live upon the earth. However, we have our own responsibilities in this matter. There are certain principles given in Scripture that, when applied, may lead to a longer life. Hence, respecting the Lord and His commandments can lead to a long life.

On the other hand, if we persist in certain sins, especially of a public nature, this may lead the Lord to take us home prematurely. There are a number of illustrations of this in Scripture.

In the Old Testament, King Saul of Israel was rejected by the Lord because he did not obey God's instructions. Instead of looking to the Lord for guidance, Saul went his own way. Eventually he consulted a medium, a witch. This act of defiance to the specific commandment of the Lord cost Saul his life. He died in battle. This did not have to happen.

In the New Testament, we find two characters, Ananias and Sapphira, who were struck down with death because they publicly lied to the apostles of Christ.

The death of these two individuals caused fear to enter into the hearts of the early believers. They realized that lying to God was a terrible thing.

The Bible also says that certain believers in the city of Corinth died prematurely through disobedience. In these instances, their disobedience was public. They were abusing the Lord's Supper. This was a solemn event. However, all could see what they were doing and God would not allow this type of public disobedience.

It is important for us to realize what these disobedient New Testament believers lost. It was their physical lives. They did not lose their eternal salvation. They were judged for their disobedience but the punishment was not everlasting separation from the Lord.

Instead, they were taken to heaven prematurely. In other words, they could have lived many more years here upon the earth in service to the

Lord. However, their disobedience necessitated the Lord taking them home early.

This illustrates that sin does have its consequences. We cannot expect to be blessed of God if we persist in certain types of sin. Consequently, our behavior does matter.

QUESTION 25

Burial Or Cremation?
What Should The Christian Do?

As we noted in earlier questions, (10-11), in ancient Israel burial was the norm for the people of God. Cremation was not an option.

This brings us to the issue of cremation in our present day. Are there any guidelines for Christians to follow? What should we do with the body of a believer who has died? Should we bury it? Should we cremate it?

Should we request to be buried or cremated when we die? Does the Bible have anything specifically to say about this issue? Does it really matter what we do? Is there a "Christian" answer to this question?

OPTION 1: WHY BURIAL OF THE DEAD IS PREFERRED

Many Bible-believers are opposed to cremating the dead. While there is nothing in the Scripture that strictly prohibits cremation, they believe that there are a number of reasons as to why cremation is not the best way for the Christian to treat the body of the believer who has died. Usually, the reasons given for this belief are as follows.

REASON 1: THE EXAMPLE OF BIBLICAL CHARACTERS

As we have already seen, the Bible consistently records that the bodies of believers were buried upon death. Indeed, there is no recorded occurrence in Scripture where the body of a believer in the God of the Bible was purposely burned or cremated instead of being buried.

While burial is never directly commanded in Scripture, these illustrations of the burial of the dead may provide a pattern for us to follow.

Abraham, for example, was promised by the Lord that he would live to a ripe old age and that he would be buried. The Bible says.

> Abraham breathed his last and died in a good old age, an old man and full of years, and was gathered to his people. Isaac and Ishmael his sons buried him in the cave of Machpelah (Genesis 25:8-9 ESV).

In this case, burial was associated with the blessings of God.

REASON 2: THE LORD HIMSELF BURIED MOSES INSTEAD OF CREMATING HIM

We have also observed that the Lord Himself buried the body of Moses in a secret location. The Bible explains what happened in this manner.

> So Moses the servant of the LORD died there in the land of Moab, as the LORD had said. He buried him in the valley in the land of Moab facing Beth-peor, and no one to this day knows where his grave is (Deuteronomy 34:5-6 HCSB).

This illustration may be instructive. If the Lord merely wanted nothing to remain of the body of Moses, He could have ordered it burned. However, He did not. The Lord made certain it was buried. This is seemingly another indication that burial was seen as superior to cremation.

REASON 3: BURNING IS A SIGN OF JUDGMENT IN SCRIPTURE

Not only is burial viewed as a sign of favor, as we have seen in Scripture, the burning of the body is always found in some context of judgment. It is never equated with the normal disposition of the dead. This is a further indication that cremation was not an option for believers in biblical times.

REASON 4: JESUS, OUR EXAMPLE, WAS BURIED

New Testament believers are commanded to follow the example of
Jesus Christ. We read in First John about how we are to pattern our
lives.

> Whoever claims to live in him must walk as Jesus did (1 John
> 2:6 NIV).

We are to follow His example in all things. This example, it is contended, should include burial. Since the body of Jesus was buried, we
should also bury the dead to follow His example.

REASON 5: THE BODY MAY SEND THE WRONG MESSAGE

One of the reasons why cremation is not the preferred way in which
to deal with a dead body is the message which it may send. Indeed,
Scripture tells us that those who have believed in Jesus Christ have
escaped the burning punishment of the Lake of Fire. Indeed, we read
of what awaits the wicked in the Book of Revelation.

> And I saw the dead, great and small, standing before the
> throne, and books were opened. Also another book was
> opened, the book of life. And the dead were judged accord-
> ing to their works, as recorded in the books. And the sea
> gave up the dead that were in it, Death and Hades gave up
> the dead that were in them, and all were judged according
> to what they had done. Then Death and Hades were thrown
> into the lake of fire. This is the second death, the lake of fire;
> and anyone whose name was not found written in the book
> of life was thrown into the lake of fire (Revelation 20:12-15
> NRSV)

The wicked will experience the everlasting fire of judgment. This is
their eternal destiny for rejecting the truth of God. Why, it is argued,
should a Christian who has escaped the burning fires of hell have their

body burned upon death? It seems inconsistent with the message we are proclaiming. Therefore, the burning of a dead body of a believer sends the wrong message.

REASON 6: BURIAL IS A SIGN OF HOPE

Finally, those who have trusted Jesus Christ believe in a future resurrection of the body. The burial of a body illustrates that hope. The Apostle Paul used the illustration of planting a seed into the ground. He put it this way.

> But someone will ask, "How are the dead raised? With what kind of body do they come?" You foolish person! What you sow does not come to life unless it dies. And what you sow is not the body that is to be, but a bare kernel, perhaps of wheat or of some other grain. . . . So is it with the resurrection of the dead. What is sown is perishable; what is raised is imperishable. It is sown in dishonor; it is raised in glory. It is sown in weakness; it is raised in power. It is sown a natural body; it is raised a spiritual body. If there is a natural body, there is also a spiritual body (1 Corinthians 15:35-37, 42-45 ESV).

Therefore, burial can be viewed as an act of faith. It illustrates the hope that something infinitely better awaits the dead in Christ.

Undeniably, the hope of the believer in Jesus Christ is the resurrection of the body. Cremation does not illustrate this hope.

These are some of the reasons as to why many Christians prefer burial over cremation.

OPTION 2: WHY SOME CHRISTIANS PREFER CREMATION

If the Bible consistently records the fact that those who had died as believers were buried, then why are there Christians who choose to cremate their loved ones, or choose cremation for themselves, rather than choosing burial?

As is the case for those Christians who prefer burial, there are reasons why other believers choose cremation. Some are economic, some are practical, and some may be spiritual. We can list them as follows.

REASON 1: IT IS THE WISH OF THE DEAD PERSON

In certain cases, the reason a body of a believer is cremated does not have to do with the living as much as it does with the person who has died. He or she has previously instructed their relatives that they want their body cremated rather than buried. In these instances, those who are living have no real option but to honor the request of the deceased.

REASON 2: IT IS LESS EXPENSIVE

One major reason for choosing cremation over burial is financial. It is much cheaper to cremate a body than to bury it. Since burial would create a financial hardship to the family, cremation is chosen as a less expensive option. Therefore, in many cases, economics plays a major role as to whether someone is buried or cremated.

REASON 3: IT IS EASIER EMOTIONALLY FOR THE LIVING

There is also an emotional aspect to cremation which is not found in burial. In one sense, it finalizes the life of the person. There is nothing left of the body, no grave to visit, no place where the dead person resides. There is nothing to remind the living that this person is not with us. This may make it easier for the living to move on with their lives.

REASON 4: IT MAY NOT BE PRACTICAL TO BURY THE DEAD

In a few countries, burial is not practical. The land is so densely populated that there is no room to bury the bodies of the dead. Therefore, of necessity, the dead are cremated. This, however, is not the case for most of the world.

REASON 5: IT IS A NON-ISSUE IN OUR MODERN WORLD

This brings us to another guiding factor in the decision to prefer cremation rather than burial. Many Christians think that it does not actually matter what happens to the body of the deceased. Indeed, they never really give it a second thought.

While they may understand that burial was important in the ancient world, and it sent a message to Israel's neighbors of a hope for an eventual resurrection, the stigma with cremation is not the same in our world today. They contend that hardly anyone nowadays would assume that cremation means lack of hope for a future resurrection of the body. Thus it is a non-issue.

REASON 6: BURIAL IS NEVER COMMANDED IN SCRIPTURE

Although burial was the norm in the ancient world for the people of God, there is no specific command in the Bible to bury the dead. The fact that burial is never commanded in Scripture, for the New Testament believer, allows the modern Christian freedom in this matter.

In addition, while it was important to bury those who had died in the Promised Land, the land of Israel, we are not necessarily to assume that it should be the same outside of the Holy Land.

REASON 7: CREMATION WILL NOT HINDER THE EVENTUAL RESURRECTION OF THE BODY

Moreover, while we know the Lord will resurrect the dead bodies of believers, after a period of time there is little, if anything, left of the dead person who is buried. As Scripture says, we all go back to the dust. Therefore, the miracle of the resurrection of the body will not necessarily be made easier by burial rather than by cremation.

Furthermore, there is something else we must remember about the Lord. He asks this question.

I am the LORD, the God of all mankind. Is anything too hard for me? (Jeremiah 32:27 NIV).

NOTHING IS TOO DIFFICULT FOR HIM. NOTHING!

Some translations render this verse as a statement rather than a question. For example, the New English Translation says.

> I am the LORD, the God of all humankind. There is, indeed, nothing too difficult for me (Jeremiah 32:27 NET)

Whether a question or a statement it is clear what this verse is expressing. We know that the Lord is certainly able to raise the bodies of the dead believers; whether buried or cremated. Indeed, nothing is too difficult for Him!

REASON 8: UNBELIEVERS WERE ALSO BURIED IN ANCIENT ISRAEL

It can also be observed that even unbelievers in ancient Israel were buried. Therefore, in those cases, it was not seen as exhibiting hope in a future resurrection in the presence of the Lord; since they would not have this hope.

In fact, the Book of Daniel makes it clear that the unbelievers would be raised to "everlasting shame."

> Many of those who sleep in the dusty ground will awake—some to everlasting life, and others to shame and everlasting abhorrence (Daniel 12:2 NET).

This being the case, the final disposition of the body becomes more of a practical issue rather than a spiritual issue.

These are some of the reasons as to why certain Bible-believers may choose to cremate their loved ones rather than burying them. Again, we stress that it is not a sin to cremate the dead. Nothing in Scripture commands that the dead should be buried.

FOR WHAT IT'S WORTH: A PERSONAL OPINION

While there does not seem to be any right or wrong way for the disposition of the body of the dead believer, if it is possible, the author thinks that the dead should be buried as a testimony to the Christian belief in the resurrection of the dead. Burial reminds us that the body and the spirit will someday be joined. This, indeed, is the hope of the believer.

Add to this, the writing on the tombstone can serve as a continual testimony that the person believed that someday they will be raised from the dead. Indeed, when one visits a cemetery it is encouraging to see all the grave markers that have words of hope for a future resurrection in Jesus Christ.

Again, there is no right or wrong answer on this question and many times the circumstances are complex. Hence, each of us must do what we feel is proper in the particular situation which we are facing.

SUMMARY TO QUESTION 25
BURIAL OR CREMATION? WHAT SHOULD THE CHRISTIAN DO?

One of the problems which Christians face is what to do with their own body when they die, as well as the bodies of believing loved ones. Should Christians who have died be buried or cremated? Does it matter? There are a number of issues which need to be looked at in answering this question.

To begin with, the New Testament does not specifically command that the dead should be buried rather than cremated. This must be clearly understood. While, in Old Testament times, those who died in the Promised Land were to be buried, we do not have any New Testament instructions as to what believers should do.

However, every example in the New Testament where there is an explanation of what happened to the body of the believer, we always find the body being buried, they are never cremated.

In addition, the few examples of bodies being burned in the Old Testament are always in a context of judgment. This ancient practice may provide us with a clue as to what we should do with the dead.

There are actually a number of reasons as to why believers choose burial over cremation. We can list them as follows.

First, the example we have of the biblical characters. Burial was the norm. Many Christians believe that we should follow their example as much as we are able.

Second, Moses' body was buried in a secret place by the Lord Himself. Evidently, it was to keep it from being used as some sort of shrine. However, while God could have easily had his body burned to accomplish the same purpose, the Lord chose not to do this. This is another indication of the superiority of burial.

As we mentioned, burning of bodies in the Scripture is always in a context of judgment. It is never looked at as an honor afforded to believers.

There is also the case of Jesus. He was buried. As our example, we should follow Him in all things. This should include burial.

Furthermore, the burning of the body of a believer can send the wrong message. Eternal punishment for the unbeliever is spoken of as fire. Indeed, the place of final judgment is called the "lake of fire." Believers have escaped the fire of judgment through belief in Jesus. Therefore, it is contended, that we should not allow our bodies to be burned upon death.

Burial also reveals a belief in the hope of a resurrection of the body. It is a testimony that we believe that someday our spirits will rejoin our bodies as our bodies are transformed by Jesus Christ into a body like His. It will be a glorified resurrected body.

In addition, our tombstone can have words of hope of our eventual resurrection from the dead. In this way, even though we have departed from this life, we are still testifying to all who read it.

This sums up some of the major arguments for burial. If there are strong reasons to bury the dead, then why do other believers allow their loved ones to be cremated as well as choosing cremation for themselves? There are a number of reasons.

At times, it is the request of the Christian who has died. Therefore, the living relatives are merely following the wishes of the dead. They really have no real choice in the matter.

Expense is sometimes an issue. Since cremation is much cheaper than burial it is often chosen because of financial reasons. This is a reality in many cases.

The living may choose cremation because it is easier emotionally. Burning the body of the deceased gives a type of finality to the death process. Those who are living do not have to be worried about driving by a cemetery where the body of their loved one resides. Cremation solves this emotional issue.

In a few cases, it would not be practical to bury the dead. Because of the crowded conditions, there is not enough room to place a body in the ground. While rare, this does occur in a few counties where the population is so dense.

Finally, there are those who do not see this as an important issue. The dead are dead and it does not really matter about the final disposition of the remains. In addition, there is no longer a stigma attached to cremating a body as there was in the ancient world.

Therefore, it is contended that cremation is a viable option for the believer in Christ.

We again stress that the burial of dead believers is never specifically commanded in the New Testament.

In sum, the ultimate decision should be left up to each and every individual and we certainly should not judge another person on the decision they have made. It can indeed be a complex issue.

What Does Scripture Have To Say About Suicide?

Unhappily, every day there are people who take their own life. Young and old, rich and poor, famous and unknown, suicide takes these people from us. Does the Bible have anything to say about this subject? Are there examples in Scripture of people who have committed suicide? What, if anything, can we learn about suicide from the Bible?

There are a number of important observations which we need to make about suicide. They include the following.

1. HUMAN BEINGS ARE SPECIAL

To begin with, we must appreciate the fact that human beings are special. We have been made in the image of God. In the Book of Genesis we read about the creation of the first humans; Adam and Eve. Scripture makes it clear that we humans are indeed unique. The Bible says.

> Then God said, "Let us make humankind in our image, according to our likeness; and let them have dominion over the fish of the sea, and over the birds of the air, and over the cattle, and over all the wild animals of the earth, and over every creeping thing that creeps upon the earth." So God created humankind in his image, in the image of God he created them; male and female he created them (Genesis 1:26-27 NRSV).

Only humans have been created in the image of God. Hence, the Lord has made us distinct from the animal kingdom. Human life is special; more important than all other types of life. This is the consistent teaching of Scripture.

2. ONLY GOD CAN TAKE A HUMAN LIFE

Because human life is special, only God has the right to take someone's life. In the Book of Deuteronomy we read the Lord saying the following to the people.

> See now that I myself am He! There is no god besides me. I put to death and I bring to life, I have wounded and I will heal, and no one can deliver out of my hand (Deuteronomy 32:39 NIV).

He is the One who makes these decisions, it should not be us. Indeed, it should NEVER be us!

In the Book of Job we find Job realizing that the Lord gives life and the Lord takes away life. He put it this way.

> He [Job] said, "Naked I came from my mother's womb, and naked shall I return there; the LORD gave, and the LORD has taken away; blessed be the name of the LORD" (Job 1:21 NRSV).

God, and God alone, has authority over human life. Scripture is very clear on this matter.

3. SUICIDE IS MURDER

The next point we learn is that suicide is murder. The Bible says that we are not to murder anyone. In the Ten Commandments it says the following.

> You shall not murder (Exodus 20:13 ESV).

This includes murdering yourself. Suicide is self-murder.

THE BIBLE GIVES A NUMBER OF EXAMPLES OF SUICIDE

Scripture gives a number of examples of people committing suicide. They are as follows.

EXAMPLE 1: ABIMELECH

In the Book of Judges, there is the record of a man named Abimelech who committed suicide. He asked for his armor bearers to kill him rather than suffering the fate of being killed by a woman. Scripture records it this way.

> And a certain woman threw an upper millstone on Abimelech's head and crushed his skull. Then he called quickly to the young man his armor-bearer and said to him, "Draw your sword and kill me, lest they say of me, 'A woman killed him.' And his young man thrust him through, and he died" (Judges 9:53-54 ESV).

This is the first recorded suicide in Scripture; though Abimelech had his armor bearer do the deed that he was too weak to do.

EXAMPLE 2: SAUL AND HIS ARMOR BEARER

The Bible also records the suicide of King Saul and his armor bearer. We read the following.

> When the battle intensified against Saul, the archers caught up with him and severely wounded him. Then Saul said to his armor-bearer, "Draw your sword and run me through with it, or these uncircumcised men will come and run me through and torture me." But his armor-bearer would not do it because he was terrified. Then Saul took his sword and fell on it. When his armor-bearer saw that Saul was dead, he also fell on his own sword and died with him" (1 Samuel 31:3-5 HCSB).

This is a case of double-suicide. Saul would rather commit suicide than fall into the hands of his enemies. Therefore, he took his own life and his armor bearer did the same.

EXAMPLE 3: KING ZIMRI OF ISRAEL

There was also a suicide by a man named Zimri who was one of the kings of ancient Israel. Scripture puts it this way.

> When Zimri saw that the city was taken, he went into the citadel of the royal palace and set the palace on fire around him. So he died, because of the sins he had committed, doing evil in the eyes of the LORD and walking in the ways of Jeroboam and in the sin he had committed and had caused Israel to commit (1 Kings 16:18-19 NIV).

Zimri burned himself with fire in his royal palace. He was an evil king who did not walk in the ways of the Lord.

EXAMPLE 4: AHITHOPHEL THE ADVISOR TO DAVID

Ahithophel was the advisor to King David. When the king did not listen to his advice but rather to the advice of another advisor, Ahithophel decided to take his own life. The Bible records what occurred as follows.

> When Ahithophel saw that his advice had not been followed, he saddled his donkey and set out for his house in his hometown. He put his house in order and then hanged himself. So he died and was buried in his father's tomb (2 Samuel 17:23 NIV).

The fact that his advice was not followed by King David led Ahithophel to kill himself.

EXAMPLE 5: THE TRAITOR JUDAS

There is also the infamous incident of the turncoat Judas hanging himself after betraying Jesus Christ. The Bible says the traitor met his demise in the following manner.

And throwing down the pieces of silver into the temple, he
departed, and he went and hanged himself (Matthew 27:5
ESV).

Judas decided to end his own life.

OBSERVATIONS ON THOSE WHO TOOK THEIR OWN LIFE

From looking at the totality of Scripture, we can make a number of
observations on the subject of the Bible and suicide. They are as follows.

1. SUICIDE WAS NOT THAT FREQUENT

First, Scripture lists only a few examples of people taking their own
lives. This gives the indication that suicide was something which was
infrequent for the nation Israel.

2. IT WAS NOT SEEN AS SOMETHING NOBLE

Not only was suicide infrequent, there is never the slightest indication
that those who committed suicide did something noble. Never do we
find the Lord commending their actions.

3. THE PEOPLE WHOSE SUICIDE WAS RECORDED WERE CAST IN AN EVIL LIGHT

In addition, each person who committed suicide is portrayed in
Scripture as either an evil character, or one who did an evil deed. There
are never looked upon as spiritual giants.

EXAMPLES OF THOSE WHO WANTED THEIR LIFE OVER BUT DID NOT CONTEMPLATE SUICIDE

In contrast to those who committed suicide, the Bible gives three specific examples of people who certainly wanted to die but did not even
contemplate taking their own lives. These examples are highly instructive. They are as follows.

EXAMPLE 1: JONAH

The prophet Jonah was very upset that God did not destroy the evil city of Nineveh. In fact, he was irritated to the point that he wanted God to take his life. In his exasperation, Jonah said the following to the Lord.

> Just kill me now, LORD! I'd rather be dead than alive because nothing I predicted is going to happen (Jonah 4:3 NLT).

Although Jonah wanted to die, suicide was never an option for him. Never do we find him attempting to take his own life. Rather he asked the Lord to take it from him. He realized that only God had the right to do this.

EXAMPLE 2: ELIJAH

The prophet Elijah was depressed. He was running away from Queen Jezebel who wanted to kill him. We read the following account of what occurred.

> Ahab told Jezebel all that Elijah had done, and how he had killed all the prophets with the sword. Then Jezebel sent a messenger to Elijah, saying, "So may the gods do to me, and more also, if I do not make your life like the life of one of them by this time tomorrow." Then he was afraid; he got up and fled for his life, and came to Beer-sheba, which belongs to Judah; he left his servant there. But he himself went a day's journey into the wilderness, and came and sat down under a solitary broom tree. He asked that he might die: "It is enough; now, O LORD, take away my life, for I am no better than my ancestors" (1 Kings 19:1-4 NRSV)

Again, we find a man wanting to die but asking the Lord to take his life. There is no indication whatsoever that Elijah desired to end his life by his own hand. He realized only the Lord had the right to do this.

EXAMPLE 3: JOB

The patriarch Job suffered greatly. He not only regretted the day of his birth but he wanted his life to end. He said.

> I'd rather choke to death than live in this body (Job 7:15 CEV).

Yet with all of his suffering, suicide was not an option for Job. It was never attempted or contemplated.

In each of these examples the biblical character wished to die. However, they realized that life is a gift from God. It is not something that we have the right to end. God gives life and God takes it away. Those who commit suicide are playing God. This is something which nobody should ever do.

Therefore, for the believer in Jesus Christ suicide should NEVER be seen as a noble option. It is not. In fact, it should never be viewed as any option.

SUMMARY TO QUESTION 26
WHAT DOES SCRIPTURE HAVE TO SAY ABOUT SUICIDE?

Unhappily, every day there are people who take their own life. For whatever reason, they decide to end it all as far as this life is concerned. This being the case, it is vital to know what the Bible has to say about suicide. How does Scripture view someone who takes their own life? Are they seen as doing a noble deed? Should a Christian see this as an option?

It is important that we first note that human life is something very special. The Bible says that we are different from all other creatures that have been created because we alone have been made in the image of God. Because human life is sacred, only God has the right to take it. Therefore, we have no right to kill ourselves. Doing so is murder.

There are examples of suicide which are recorded in Scripture. When we look at these various accounts there are a number of conclusions we can make.

First, we find that suicide is rare. In fact, the Bible provides only five cases of people committing suicide. They are a man named Abimelech, King Saul and his armor bearer, David's advisor Ahithophel, an evil king of Israel named Zimri, and the most famous of all, the betrayer of Jesus, Judas Iscariot.

When we look at what the Bible has to say about these men we discover that suicide is never viewed as something noble. Indeed, the description which the Bible gives of them taking their life casts them all in a bad light. There was nothing heroic about what they did.

From looking at the biblical evidence we conclude that suicide is not something that is ever looked upon in a favorable manner. It is always a tragic event. There are no winners when someone commits suicide.

There is something else we discover. There were three biblical characters, Jonah, Elijah and Job, which wanted their life to end because of the difficult circumstances in which they found themselves. However, *none* of them attempted suicide or even contemplated it. These men of God realized that God alone has the right to take a human life, even our own lives. Suicide never entered the picture.

This is a further indication that suicide should never be seen as an option for the believer. It is not a choice which anyone who believes in Jesus Christ should contemplate.

How Shall We View Samson Taking His Own Life? Did He Commit Suicide?

Suicide in Scripture is never viewed as something which is honorable or noble. It is not something for which people are accorded any great honor or are applauded for doing so. Each situation was tragic.

This brings up the question of the Judge Samson. The Bible says that he took his own life by pulling down the columns of a building which was filled with the enemies of Israel, the Philistines. Scripture records it this way.

> Samson told the young man who was leading him by the hand, "Let me rest. Let me touch the columns on which the building stands so that I can lean against them." The building was filled with people. All the Philistine rulers were there. On the roof there were about three thousand men and women who watched Samson entertain them Then Samson called to the LORD, "Almighty LORD, please remember me! God, give me strength just one more time! Let me get even with the Philistines for at least one of my two eyes." Samson felt the two middle columns on which the building stood. With his right hand on one column and his left on the other, he pushed hard against them. "Let me die with the Philistines," he said. With that, he pushed with all his might, and the building fell on the rulers and everyone in it. So he

killed more Philistines when he died than he had when he was alive (Judges 16:26-30 God's Word).

Was this suicide? If so, then why did God give Samson the strength to do it if suicide is a sin? How do we explain what happened?

In looking at the story of Samson there are a number of observations which need to be made.

1. GOD GAVE HIM THE STRENGTH TO PULL DOWN THE BUILDING

To begin with, we must note that it was the Lord Himself who answered Samson's prayer and gave him his supernatural strength back. Therefore, what Samson did was not a sin. God would never participate in sin.

2. SAMSON SACRIFICED HIS LIFE FOR OTHERS

This brings us to our next point. Samson did not kill himself because he was distressed with his life. He actually sacrificed his life in destroying many of God's enemies, the Philistines. Samson died so that others might not have to die. This is *not* suicide.

3. JESUS LAID DOWN HIS LIFE FOR OTHERS

Scripture actually commends a person who will lay down their life for someone else. The Apostle Paul wrote to the Romans about what Jesus did on our behalf.

> For while we were still weak, at the right time Christ died for the ungodly. Indeed, rarely will anyone die for a righteous person-- though perhaps for a good person someone might actually dare to die. But God proves his love for us in that while we still were sinners Christ died for us (Romans 5:6-8 NRSV)

The translation God's Word puts it in this manner.

Look at it this way: At the right time, while we were still helpless, Christ died for ungodly people. Finding someone who would die for a godly person is rare. Maybe someone would have the courage to die for a good person. Christ died for us while we were still sinners. This demonstrates God's love for us (Romans 5:6-8 God's Word).

Hence, Jesus Christ died for the human race even though all of us were in rebellion against Him. This demonstrates the great love He has for us.

Jesus Himself spoke of laying down His life for His sheep. John records Him saying the following words.

I am the good shepherd. The good shepherd gives His life for the sheep . . . Therefore My Father loves Me, because I lay down My life that I may take it again (John 10:11,17 NKJV)

Jesus, the Good Shepherd, died for His sheep, the believers. In fact, Jesus testified that God the Father loved Him for doing so.

In addition, Jesus also said that a person can show no greater love than to die for someone else. He put it this way.

Greater love has no one than this, that he lay down his life for his friends (John 15:13 NIV)

Again, our Lord demonstrated that great love by going to the cross at Calvary and dying in our place.

The New Testament makes it clear that the purpose of the coming of Christ into the world was to offer His life on behalf of others. Matthew wrote about this important truth. He put it this way.

It's the same way with the Son of Man. He didn't come so that others could serve him. He came to serve and to give his life as a ransom for many people (Matthew 20:28 God's Word)

In sum, sacrificing our life for the sake of others is not suicide. While some people put Samson in the category of those who committed suicide, this is not the case at all. Rather he should be seen as a warrior who took the lives of many of the enemies of God in his death. His act was noble.

SUMMARY TO QUESTION 27
HOW SHALL WE VIEW SAMSON TAKING HIS OWN LIFE? DID HE COMMIT SUICIDE?

The biblical character Samson lived an inconsistent life. On too many occasions he failed to properly use the supernatural strength which the Lord gave him.

In fact, his life ended when he took his own life by pulling down a building filled with the enemies of Israel, the Philistines. Though some consider this an act of suicide, it was truly a heroic deed. Samson actually killed more of the evil Philistines in his death than he did in his entire life.

There are several things we need to understand about what happened to Samson and the entire subject of suicide.

For one thing, it was the Lord who gave Samson the strength to do this task. At that time, Samson had lost his supernatural strength. In an answer to his prayer, the great strength returned to destroy the Philistines. Thus, the Lord is the One who empowered Samson.

Rather than seeing this as a suicide, the act of Samson should be seen as a deed which saved the lives of others. It is similar to a soldier throwing himself upon a live grenade to save the lives of his fellow soldiers. Samson saved a number of Israelite lives by his act. He was a hero.

Giving our lives for the sake of others is a biblical principle. Indeed, this was the main purpose of Jesus coming to the earth. He died so that others may live. He gave His life for the sake of others.

This is the main point of the message of the gospel. We are not able to save ourselves but Jesus can save us if we will allow Him to do it. He died so that we can live.

Consequently, the act of Samson should be seen the same way; though on a much smaller scale. Samson did not commit suicide.

QUESTION 28

Do Those Who Commit Suicide Automatically Go To Hell? (1 Corinthians 3:16-17) Is It The Unpardonable Sin?

Suicide is tragic. Whenever someone takes their own life it hurts everyone associated with that person. There are no exceptions. There are no winners.

One of the questions which often arises about those who have committed suicide concerns their eternal destiny. Do Christians automatically go to hell because they have taken their own life? A number of people think that this is the case. Several arguments are given for this position. They include the following.

SCRIPTURE SAYS GOD WILL DESTROY THOSE WHO DESTROY HIS TEMPLE

A passage which is used as support for this belief is found in First Corinthians 3:16-17. Paul wrote the following words to the church at Corinth.

> Do you not know that you are God's temple and that God's Spirit dwells in you? If anyone destroys God's temple, God will destroy him. For God's temple is holy, and you are that temple (1 Corinthians 3:16-17 ESV).

This passage is used as a proof-text for the ultimate fate of those who take their own life. Our bodies are the temple of the Holy Spirit. If we destroy our body, then God will destroy us. This is understood to mean that we will lose any hope of being with Him in eternity. Suicide, it is argued, will keep someone out of heaven.

2. A PERSON CANNOT CONFESS THE SIN OF SUICIDE

Another argument for suicide being a reason to send someone straight to hell concerns the lack of the possibility of repentance. If a person takes their own life they cannot later confess this sin. By definition, this is their last act.

3. SUICIDE IS MURDER

Suicide is murder. In the Ten Commandments we read.

You shall not murder (Exodus 20:13 NIV)

This includes murdering or killing yourself! Consequently, when a person commits suicide they die with unconfessed sin, the sin of murdering oneself. This is another reason why some people consider suicide as the unpardonable sin. Indeed, how can God allow a person to enter His holy presence when their last act upon the earth was committing murder?

These are some of the reasons as to why many people assume that suicide will keep people out of heaven.

RESPONSE: SUICIDE CAN BE FORGIVEN

While there are those who believe suicide is the unforgivable sin, Scripture does not teach this. There are a number of points which we need to make.

THE BLASPHEMY AGAINST THE HOLY SPIRIT IS THE ONLY UNPARDONABLE SIN

To begin with, the Lord Jesus said that the only sin which could not be forgiven was blasphemy against the Holy Spirit. We read His words in Matthew's gospel.

Therefore I tell you, every sin and blasphemy will be forgiven people, but the blasphemy against the Spirit will not be forgiven. And whoever speaks a word against the Son of Man will be forgiven, but whoever speaks against the Holy Spirit will not be forgiven, either in this age or in the age to come (Matthew 12:31-32 ESV).

According to Jesus there is one, and only one, sin which will not be forgiven. This sin is the blasphemy against the Holy Spirit. Everything else will be forgiven. Everything!

We will look at what it means to "blaspheme the Holy Spirit" in our next two questions and we will discover that it is NOT suicide. Simply stated, blasphemy against the Holy Spirit is the continual rejection of Jesus Christ as Savior. This is the one sin for which there is no forgiveness. Suicide can be forgiven.

THE MENTAL STATE OF THE PERSON NEEDS TO BE CONSIDERED

There is something else. Often when people commit suicide it is because of their fragile or compromised mental state. Many factors can be involved. Illness, depression, and senility can all contribute to someone taking their own life. Certainly a person who is not "in their right mind" cannot be held responsible for acts they otherwise would not do. This occurs frequently in people who commit suicide.

In addition, many people commit suicide on the spur of the moment. Something usually takes place, which is so horrific in their mind, that it causes the immediate unplanned action of taking their own life.

Paul Was Not Speaking To The Individual (1 Corinthians 3:16,17)

Now we consider the Scripture. In the passage recorded in First Corinthians, the subject is not the individual but rather the entire church. The word "you" in this verse is not singular but rather it is plural.

It is true that each individual believer is a temple of the Holy Spirit. Paul later wrote.

> Or do you not know that your body is a temple of the Holy Spirit within you, whom you have from God? You are not your own (1 Corinthians 6:19 ESV).

However, in the reference in 1 Corinthians 3:16-17, the individual is not in view, it is the church, the community of believers which Paul is referring to. If anyone attempts to destroy the work of God which is being carried out through the church, then God will destroy that person. The idea is that those who actively oppose the work of God will be judged. The subject of suicide is not at all what Paul is addressing here.

MANY PEOPLE DIE WITH UNCONFESSED SIN

Finally, there is the case of people dying with unconfessed sin. Obviously a person cannot repent or confess the sin of committing suicide. Yet we must realize that there are a number of sins which all of us commit which we do not confess. What if a person goes to bed angry at a husband, a wife, a father or a mother? This is sinful.

Are we to assume that if they die during the night they would go to hell because of unconfessed sin? Examples like this can be multiplied. All of us have unconfessed sin. There are no exceptions to this.

THERE ARE ALSO "SINS OF OMISSION"

There is something else. Sin not only consists of doing the wrong thing, it also consists of not doing the right thing. Undoubtedly there are many things each day that we should have done which we did not do. These are sins. Now we may not realize that it is sin but it is sin nonetheless.

Furthermore, it is unconfessed sin. Again, each of us goes to sleep each night with certain things unconfessed. These unconfessed sins do not keep us out of heaven. Jesus has died for all of our sins, past, present, and future. He has taken the punishment for these sins upon Himself whether or not we have confessed them.

Therefore, those who commit suicide do not necessarily go to hell. We say "necessarily" because the determination of who gets into heaven, and who does not, is based upon what a person does with Jesus Christ. Those who believe in Him are going to heaven when they die. Those who do not are going to hell.

THERE ARE NO WINNERS IN SUICIDE

We again must stress the fact that suicide is an extremely selfish act. There are no winners when a person takes their own life. It leaves behind shattered lives of those who loved that person.

Consequently, as we indicated in a previous question, the act of suicide is neither noble nor honorable. It should never be contemplated by a child of God. Never!

SUMMARY TO QUESTION 28
DO THOSE WHO COMMIT SUICIDE AUTOMATICALLY GO TO HELL? IS IT THE UNPARDONABLE SIN?

There are some Christians who assume that when a believer in Jesus Christ commits suicide it automatically sends them to hell. A number of arguments are usually made for this position.

One passage which is often used is 1 Corinthians 3:16-17. It says that the Lord will destroy those who destroy God's temple. This has been understood to mean that anyone who takes their own life will not be allowed to enter heaven. Since our body is called the temple of the Holy Spirit, we will be destroyed if we destroy the temple.

There is also the issue of unconfessed sin in our lives. By definition, suicide is not a sin from which we can later repent. Since those who die by means of suicide were not able to confess their sins it is assumed by some that they will not be allowed to enter heaven.

In addition, suicide is murder. Are we to assume that the Lord will let a person into heaven whose last act is murder? Thus, many people conclude that suicide keeps people from entering heaven since it is the unpardonable sin.

But this is not the case. Suicide, by itself, will not keep one from heaven. The only unforgivable sin is the blasphemy against the Holy Spirit. Today this consists of rejecting the work of the Holy Spirit which convicts a person of sin and their need of Christ as Savior. If a person rejects this work of the Spirit of God, then there can be no forgiveness. Everything else can be forgiven. This includes suicide.

The mental state of the person also has to be considered. Indeed, often those who commit suicide have some type of mental illness or instability where they are not acting rationally. Others commit suicide on the spur of the moment when something tragic occurs in their life. These circumstances need to be appreciated by those who want to automatically consign someone to hell who takes their own life.

In addition, the passage in First Corinthians is not speaking of individual believers. The word "you" is plural. The passage is emphasizing that God will judge those people who attempt to stop His ongoing work through His temple on the earth, His church. It is not addressing individual believers who take their own lives. The subject of suicide is not being addressed in this passage.

Finally, we all have unconfessed sin. We go to sleep each night with these sins. Indeed, none of us confess everything which we have done sinful on that particular day.

In addition, there are also sins of omission on our part. There are certain things which we should have done which we do not do. These acts are sinful but they are hardly ever confessed by us.

Fortunately this lack of confession will not keep us out of God's kingdom. Jesus Christ has taken the penalty of our sins upon Himself. Once we trust Him as Savior we are forgiven for all of our sins. This includes future sins.

Thus, the lack of confession of a particular sin which we did do, or something which we should have done which we did not do, will not keep us out of heaven.

We therefore conclude that suicide, by itself, does not keep one out of heaven. What keeps a person out of heaven is rejecting Jesus Christ as their Savior. This is the unforgivable sin.

Having said this we again must stress that suicide is a selfish act and always leads to horrific pain and suffering for those left behind. While it may be forgiven, it should never be seen as an option for those who believe in Christ.

QUESTION 29

What Is The Blasphemy Against The Holy Spirit? (Why Is This The Unpardonable Sin?)

Suicide is not the unpardonable sin. As tragic as it is, this does not mean the person automatically goes to hell. However, there is an unpardonable sin that will keep people out of heaven. Since this is the teaching of Scripture, we need to understand exactly what it is so that we will not commit it.

In this question, we will examine what exactly the unpardonable sin was in Jesus' day. In our next question, we will discover what the unpardonable sin is in our present day.

THE CONFRONTATION OF JESUS WITH THE RELIGIOUS LEADERS

During His earthly ministry, in a confrontation with the religious rulers, the Lord Jesus spoke of an unforgivable sin called the "blasphemy against the Holy Spirit." He said that whoever commits this terrible sin would never be forgiven. Indeed, they could not be forgiven in this life or in the next. Since there is such a thing as an "unforgivable sin," that will keep people out of heaven, it is vital that we know exactly what this sin is.

WHAT DOES IT MEAN TO BLASPHEME?

To begin with, it is important that we understand what is meant by the term "blasphemy." Basically it has the idea to "speak against, insult, or curse." In Scripture, the word is used for insults hurled at both God and humans.

For example, the Greek noun "blaspheme" is used of people slandering one another. Paul used it in his letter to the Ephesians. He encouraged the believers not to "slander" others. He put it this way.

> All bitterness, anger and wrath, insult and slander must be removed from you, along with all wickedness (Ephesians 4:31 HCSB).

The word translated as "slander" is the Greek word "blaspheme." In this context, it speaks of insults or curses one person directs at another. Paul said that this is something which believers should not do. Thus, blasphemies, slanderous or insulting accusations, can be directed at people.

The word translated blasphemy can also be used of strong insults or curses directed against God. Scripture records a number of examples of people cursing the God of the Bible.

The people of Israel who left Egypt in the Exodus were accused of insulting or blaspheming God. Indeed, not only did they build a golden calf, they claimed that this image was the actual god which brought them out of the land of Egypt! Scripture says.

> Even when they had made for themselves a golden calf and said, 'This is your God who brought you up out of Egypt, and had committed great blasphemies' (Nehemiah 9:18 ESV).

These acts by the people were considered insults or blasphemies against God.

In fact, we find that Jesus Himself was accused of blasphemy by the religious rulers. He claimed the ability, or the right, to be able to forgive sins. Yet this was something which God alone could do. We read the following response of the religious leaders to Jesus' claim to forgive the sins of a certain paralyzed man.

> Why does this Man speak blasphemies like this? Who can forgive sins but God alone? (Mark 2:7 NKJV).

They realized that God alone forgive sins. Consequently, they assumed Jesus was blaspheming or insulting God by claiming the same authority.

Therefore, the word is not a special term which refers to cursing or insulting God. Instead, the context must determine whether the insult or curse is against God or another human being.

CURSING GOD WAS A SERIOUS OFFENSE

In the Old Testament, we find that cursing or insulting God was an extremely serious offence. Those who openly defied the Lord were to be cut off from the people. Scripture says.

> But anyone who sins defiantly, whether native-born or for-eigner, blasphemes the LORD and must be cut off from their people. Because they have despised the LORD's word and broken his commands, they must surely be cut off; their guilt remains on them (Numbers 15:30-31 NIV).

Notice this includes native-born Israelites as well as foreigners. Anyone who blasphemes the Lord was to be cut off from the people.

In another place, we read that those who cursed the Lord were worthy of the death penalty. Moses wrote.

> And speak to the people of Israel, saying, Whoever curses his God shall bear his sin. Whoever blasphemes the name of the LORD shall surely be put to death. All the congregation shall stone him. The sojourner as well as the native, when he blasphemes the Name, shall be put to death (Leviticus 24:15-16 NIV).

Therefore, simply stated, the blasphemy against the Holy Spirit would involve some type of insulting, or cursing, the work of the Holy Spirit. The Jewish audience which Jesus addressed certainly knew the serious nature of such a sin.

THE BACKGROUND OF JESUS' STATEMENT

This brings us to the setting, or occasion, of Jesus' statement. The background of Jesus' statement can be found in Matthew 12:22-30. Jesus healed a man who was possessed by a demon. His demon possession made him blind, mute, and probably deaf. This combination of illnesses made it impossible for anyone to cast the demon out of the man because there was no way anyone could communicate with him.

When the people saw Jesus heal the man, they wondered if He could be the long-awaited Messiah. Indeed, who else but the Messiah could perform such a miracle? However, not everyone was convinced.

THE ACCUSATION THAT WAS MADE AGAINST JESUS

The suggestion that Jesus could be the promised Messiah brought a quick response from the religious leaders. Matthew records the following.

> But when the Pharisees heard it, they said, "It is only by Beelzebul, the prince of demons, that this man casts out demons" (Matthew 12:24 ESV).

They accused Jesus of casting out demons by the power of Satan. In other words, they could not deny His power but rather they attributed it to some evil or demonic source. Who would want to follow someone who is working with Satan? Since the religious leaders were supposedly in a position to determine the source of Jesus' miracles, this accusation had to be answered by the Lord.

THE RESPONSE BY JESUS: SATAN DOES NOT WORK AGAINST HIMSELF

Jesus responded by showing how illogical their arguments were. He made it clear that Satan would not cast out Satan. We read what took place.

> Since Jesus knew what they were thinking, he said to them, "Every kingdom divided against itself is ruined. And every city or household divided against itself will not last. If Satan forces Satan out, he is divided against himself. How, then, can his kingdom last? If I force demons out of people with the help of Beelzebul, who helps your followers force them out? That's why they will be your judges. But if I force demons out with the help of God's Spirit, then the kingdom of God has come to you. How can anyone go into a strong man's house and steal his property? First he must tie up the strong man. Then he can go through his house and steal his property (Matthew 12:25-29 God's Word).

Satan was not in the business of casting out himself. The power to exorcise demons belongs to God and to Him alone. The fact that Jesus could cast out demons made it plain that the power of God was operating among them. Therefore, these people were held responsible to respond to God's miraculous power in their midst.

To reject God's work among them was insulting or cursing God. It was blaspheming the work of the Holy Spirit. As we mentioned, the Old Testament prescribed the death penalty for those who did such things. Consequently, attributing Jesus' Spirit-led miracles to a demonic source was the worst sin which they could commit. Indeed, by doing so, they were cursing the God of the Bible.

JESUS' RESPONSE TO THOSE WHO COMMIT SUCH A SIN

Jesus further responded to their false accusations. Matthew, Mark and Luke record Jesus' words about the fate of those who blaspheme against the Holy Spirit. Matthew writes.

> Every sin or blasphemy can be forgiven-- except blasphemy against the Holy Spirit, which can never be forgiven. Anyone who blasphemes against me, the Son of Man, can be forgiven, but blasphemy against the Holy Spirit will never be forgiven, either in this world or in the world to come (Matthew 12:31,32 NLT).

No forgiveness is possible for those who commit this sin.

Mark records Jesus' words in this manner.

> Truly, I say to you, all sins will be forgiven the children of man, and whatever blasphemies they utter, but whoever blasphemes against the Holy Spirit never has forgiveness, but is guilty of an eternal sin— for they were saying, "He has an unclean spirit" (Mark 3:28-30 ESV).

These religious rulers attributed Jesus' exorcism to a demonic source as well as saying that He had an "unclean spirit." Mark records Jesus calling this an "eternal sin."

In another context, Luke records the following words of Jesus about the blasphemy against the Holy Spirit.

> And I tell you, everyone who acknowledges me before men, the Son of Man also will acknowledge before the angels of God, but the one who denies me before men will be denied before the angels of God. And everyone who speaks a word against the Son of Man will be forgiven, but the one who blasphemes against the Holy Spirit will not be forgiven. And when they bring you before the synagogues and the rulers and the authorities, do not be anxious about how you should defend yourself or what you should say, for the Holy Spirit will teach you in that very hour what you ought to say (Luke 12:8-12 ESV).

From these sources, we can make a number of observations from Jesus' statements about the blasphemy against the Holy Spirit.

OBSERVATION ONE: THE SIN WAS UNFORGIVABLE

First, this sin of blasphemy against the Holy Spirit was unforgivable. Matthew records Jesus saying that there would be no forgiveness in this life or in the next for what these religious leaders had done. The seriousness of their sin was made plain to them. Indeed, it would keep the offender out of heaven.

In fact, Mark records Jesus as saying that this is an "eternal sin." In other words, it has everlasting consequences. There would be no forgiveness for those who engage in such insults to God.

OBSERVATION TWO: IT SEEMS TO BE A PUBLIC REJECTION OF JESUS AND HIS MESSAGE

From Luke, we discover something else. It also seems to consist of some public rejection of the ministry of Jesus as well as that of His disciples. Indeed, in His next statement, after speaking of the blasphemy against the Holy Spirit, Jesus says that the Spirit will be with His disciples as they testify about Him before the religious authorities. It is, therefore, seemingly more than a lack of belief in Christ. It is also the public denial of the testimony of the Holy Spirit that Jesus is the Messiah, the Christ.

OBSERVATION THREE: SINS DONE IN IGNORANCE AGAINST JESUS CAN BE FORGIVEN

Interestingly, we find that Jesus said that sins against Him could be forgiven but there would be no forgiveness of those who blaspheme the Holy Spirit. This seems to mean that people could ignorantly or unintentionally say things against Jesus without committing the unpardonable sin. Forgiveness is still possible for those who do this.

However, if a person knowingly and defiantly speaks insults against the power of the Holy Spirit, who is testifying to the truth of Jesus and His message, there is no forgiveness possible. This was an especially terrible sin which the religious leaders were committing.

Indeed, they were publicly attributing Jesus' miraculous power to the devil. This was not done in ignorance. In fact, it was a willing rejection of the God of the Bible; the God whom they were supposed to be serving. Furthermore, they were doing it publicly, in front of the multitude. They were pitting their authority against His.

OBSERVATION FOUR: IT WAS AN INSULT TO GOD

Thus, specifically, in this particular context, the blasphemy against the Holy Spirit was a denial of the work of the Holy Spirit in the Person of Jesus Christ. The Holy Spirit was working in Jesus as well as through Jesus. The Spirit of God was testifying to everyone that Jesus was the Messiah. Rejecting the message of the Spirit was the same as rejecting or insulting the God of the Bible.

OBSERVATION FIVE: THEIRS WAS A CONTINUAL STATE OF SIN

There is something else we must note. These religious leaders were in a continuous state of sin by denying that the miracles of Jesus were accomplished through the power of God. Consequently they were in a constant state of sin or rebellion against God. What made matters worse was that these men were the religious authorities, the spiritual leaders. Their testimony carried great weight with the people. Their false accusations could not go unchallenged.

SUMMING IT UP: THE NATURE OF THE BLASPHEMY AGAINST THE HOLY SPIRIT

In sum, the blasphemy against the Holy Spirit, in this context, is the public attributing of the work of the Holy Spirit, through Jesus Christ, to Satan. The Holy Spirit testified of Jesus' identity as the promised

Messiah. Refusal to acknowledge this obvious testimony of the work of God was blaspheming the Holy Spirit.

This sin could not be forgiven. In other words, someone who would consciously and publicly reject that God was working through the Person of Jesus Christ, by the power of the Holy Spirit, could not be forgiven of this sin. In fact, this continual rejection of the work of the Holy Spirit is the one sin that would keep them out of heaven. All other sins could and would be forgiven.

This was what Jesus meant when He spoke of the blasphemy against the Holy Spirit. These religious leaders were committing the unpardonable sin. No forgiveness was possible as long as they were doing this.

SUMMARY TO QUESTION 29
WHAT IS THE BLASPHEMY AGAINST THE HOLY SPIRIT? (WHY IS THIS THE UNPARDONABLE SIN)

As we have noted, suicide is not the unpardonable sin. However, such a sin does exist that will keep people out of heaven.

In the gospels, we read of Jesus speaking about the "unpardonable sin." This means that there is a sin which people can commit that cannot be forgiven. It is also known as the "blasphemy against the Holy Spirit." Since this sin is unpardonable it is important that we know exactly what it is so that we do not commit it.

To begin with, we should look at what it means "to blaspheme." Blasphemy basically has the idea of insulting, cursing or speaking against someone. Depending upon the context, this insult can be directed against either humans or God. Indeed, the same word is used in Scripture of insults hurled at God as well as at other humans.

In the Old Testament, those who cursed or defiantly insulted the God of Israel were given the death penalty. Therefore, it was an especially horrific sin in God's eyes. Consequently, the people to whom Jesus spoke would be aware of the gravity of such a sin.

With this understanding of the background of the word we can have a better understanding of its meaning when Jesus used it. The context of Jesus' statement about the blasphemy against the Holy Spirit involved a certain miracle which He did. Jesus performed a mighty deed of healing a man who was demon-possessed, blind and mute. The religious leaders, instead of acknowledging Jesus as the Messiah, attributed this, as well as all of His other miracles, to the power of the devil.

Therefore, while recognizing that some power had allowed Jesus to do this miraculous work, they claimed that His power was demonic rather than the work of the Holy Spirit of God. This was not done in ignorance.

Jesus responded to their accusations. He made the statement that human beings may be forgiven for *every* sin which they commit. This includes blaspheming or insulting Christ Himself. However, there is one sin from which they can never be forgiven; the blasphemy against the Holy Spirit.

In this particular instance, the sin was attributing the work of Jesus Christ, which was done by the power of the Spirit, to the devil. In other words, it was insulting the Holy Spirit who was testifying to Christ as well as testifying through Christ.

We should note that the religious leaders were continually attributing these miraculous works of Jesus to the devil. Their verbal denouncing of Christ was public and it was ongoing. Therefore, they were consciously and knowingly rejecting the testimony of the Spirit as to the identity of Jesus Christ. The result of such insulting the Holy Spirit was that the person could not be forgiven for their sin neither in this life nor in the life to come.

In another context, Jesus used the term "blasphemy against the Holy Spirit" in reference to the message of His disciples. They preached His message with His authority. Those people who heard the message of

Jesus through the power of the Holy Spirit, but publicly and defiantly rejected it, were also guilty of committing this unpardonable sin. No forgiveness was possible for them as long as they were doing this.

Therefore, we can conclude that the blasphemy against the Holy Spirit was more than one particular sin which these religious leaders were committing. Indeed, it is a continuous state of publicly insulting or cursing the work of the Holy Spirit which was done in the Person of Christ. Since there could be no real question that the miracles of Jesus had been brought about through the power of the Holy Spirit, those who attributed His work to Satan or some demonic force could not expect to be forgiven.

Indeed, the consequences of blaspheming the Holy Spirit meant eternal damnation. There could be no forgiveness in this life or in eternity for rejecting the work of the Holy Spirit through the Person of Jesus Christ. Consequently, this is the one sin that will keep people out of heaven.

QUESTION 30

What Sin Will Keep People Out Of Heaven? How Does Someone Today Commit The Unpardonable Sin?

When Jesus Christ was on earth, He spoke of an unpardonable sin called the "blasphemy against the Holy Spirit." Jesus said this sin could not be forgiven in this life or in the next life. Indeed, it is also called an "eternal sin." Thus, committing this particular sin will keep people out of heaven.

The word blaspheme has the idea of "cursing, insulting, or rejecting." We discover that the religious leaders of His day were guilty of committing that sin. Specifically, the Holy Spirit was blasphemed when the works of Jesus Christ, performed through the power of the Holy Spirit, were attributed to the devil. Since the ministry of the Holy Spirit gave clear testimony to Jesus being the Messiah, those who rejected this truth could not be forgiven. Indeed, apart from Jesus Christ there is no forgiveness of sin.

THE IMPORTANCE OF THIS ISSUE

This brings up an all-important question. Since Jesus is no longer on the earth, then how does one blaspheme the Holy Spirit today? How does a person commit the "unpardonable sin?" In other words, what sin does a person commit that will keep them out of heaven for all eternity?

We certainly do not want to be guilty of doing this! So how can it be avoided? A number of observations need to be made in answering this crucial question.

JESUS' HISTORICAL SITUATION WAS UNIQUE

We must first understand that this particular situation, where Jesus spoke of the blasphemy against the Holy Spirit, was unique. Jesus Christ was physically present on the earth, performing miracles through the Holy Spirit's power to testify that He was the promised Messiah. The religious leaders rejected His miraculous deeds as coming from the Lord. Instead, they attributed them to a demonic source. Thus, the way in which they insulted or blasphemed the Holy Spirit was clear.

But Jesus Christ is not with us today in a physical presence like He was in the first century. Indeed, Christ is not on the earth to personally work His miracles through the power of the Holy Spirit. How then does the blasphemy against the Holy Spirit occur in our day and age without Jesus' presence? Can a person still commit the unpardonable sin?

THE WORLD STILL NEEDS FORGIVENESS

To begin with, we find that the work of the Holy Spirit is still the same. Indeed, nothing has really changed. His mission is to testify about Jesus Christ and to show the world it needs His forgiveness.

On the night of His betrayal, Jesus said the following concerning the ministry of the Holy Spirit to the unbelieving world.

> Nevertheless, I tell you the truth: it is to your advantage that I go away, for if I do not go away, the Helper will not come to you. But if I go, I will send him to you. And when he comes, he will convict the world concerning sin and righteousness and judgment: concerning sin, because they do not believe in me; concerning righteousness, because I go to the Father, and you will see me no longer; concerning judgment, because the ruler of this world is judged (John 16:7-11 ESV).

Among other things, the ministry of the Holy Spirit is to convict the unbelieving world of sin. His mission is to show them their need for Jesus Christ as Savior.

THE SIN AGAINST THE HOLY SPIRIT TODAY IS UNBELIEF IN JESUS

Therefore, the blasphemy against the Holy Spirit is unbelief in Jesus Christ. It is insulting or rejecting the work of the Holy Spirit which testifies that Christ is Savior and Lord.

This is confirmed by what Jesus said on another occasion. Indeed, He equated the blasphemy against the Holy Spirit with the preaching of the message by His disciples. We read.

> I tell you, whoever publicly acknowledges me, the Son of Man will also acknowledge before the angels of God. But whoever publicly disowns me will be disowned before the angels of God. And everyone who speaks a word against the Son of Man will be forgiven, but anyone who blasphemes against the Holy Spirit will not be forgiven. When you are brought before synagogues, rulers and authorities, do not worry about how you will defend yourselves or what you will say, for the Holy Spirit will teach you at that time what you should say (Luke 12:8-12 NIV)

The message of Jesus as the Messiah, the Christ, is still to be proclaimed today. Those who reject it are actually insulting the God of the Bible. Indeed, those who continually reject the Holy Spirit's ministry of portraying Jesus Christ as the only Savior of humanity are blaspheming the Holy Spirit. If this state of sin continues they will not receive forgiveness for their sins but rather the wrath, or judgment, of God will remain on them. The Bible makes their fate clear.

> Whoever believes in the Son has eternal life, but whoever rejects the Son will not see life, for God's wrath remains on him (John 3:36 NIV).

Those who reject God the Son, Jesus Christ, can only expect to experience God's wrath. They cannot ever receive forgiveness for their sin, neither in this world nor in the next.

IT IS A CONTINUOUS STATE OF UNBELIEF

Therefore, today, as in Christ's time, the blasphemy of the Holy Spirit is a continuous state of unbelief rather than the commission of one particular sin. Unless that state of unbelief changes, the person will suffer eternal separation from the Lord. The Bible speaks of the state of condemnation unbelievers now find themselves.

> Those who believe in him are not condemned; but those who do not believe are condemned already, because they have not believed in the name of the only Son of God (John 3:18 NRSV)

Those who have rejected Jesus Christ are in this state of unbelief. This unbelief will result in eternal condemnation unless a person turns to Christ for forgiveness.

In sum, rejecting the message of Jesus Christ is how one blasphemes the Holy Spirit in our day and age. This is the unpardonable sin which will keep people out of heaven. On the other hand, once a person trusts Christ as their Savior, then there is no possibility of them committing the unpardonable sin. Every other sin we do commit can and will be forgiven.

SUMMARY TO QUESTION 30
WHAT SIN WILL KEEP PEOPLE OUT OF HEAVEN? HOW DOES SOMEONE TODAY COMMIT THE UNPARDONABLE SIN?

During His public ministry, Jesus spoke of the sin of the blasphemy against the Holy Spirit. He referred to it as the unpardonable sin; a sin which never could be forgiven. In other words, committing this particular sin would keep people out of heaven.

In Jesus' day, the Holy Spirit testified to Him as being the promised Messiah. The miracles of Jesus were performed through the power of the Holy Spirit to give evidence of Jesus' identity. The blasphemy against the Holy Spirit consisted of attributing this particular work of the Holy Spirit to the devil. In other words, instead of acknowledging that God was with Jesus when He was doing these miracles, the religious rulers attributed His miraculous works to demonic power.

However, Jesus Christ is no longer physically present on the earth. Therefore, nobody, in exactly the same manner, can blaspheme the Holy Spirit. Indeed, nobody can attribute His miraculous works to the devil since Jesus is not with us in the same manner as He was in the first century. So can a person still blaspheme the Holy Spirit? Yes, they can.

Today one blasphemes the Holy Spirit by rejecting the ministry of the Holy Spirit that speaks of the necessity of accepting Jesus Christ as Savior. Indeed, Jesus specifically said the Holy Spirit was to come into the world and convict unbelievers of their sin. If they did not respond to His work, then there is no hope for them. There would be no forgiveness in this life or in the next.

Jesus also made this clear when He spoke of the future ministry of His disciples. Those who rejected their testimony about Jesus would also be blaspheming the Holy Spirit.

Therefore, in our day and age the blasphemy against the Holy Spirit is the state of unbelief in Jesus Christ as Savior. It is more of a continuing and persistent rejection of the Holy Spirit than one particular sin. The only way to avoid the sin of the blasphemy against the Holy Spirit is to turn to Jesus Christ for forgiveness; since apart from Him there is no forgiveness.

However, this sin cannot be committed once a person trusts Christ as Savior. Every sin we do commit will be forgiven by Him.

In sum, the only sin that will keep people out of heaven is the rejection of Jesus Christ as their Savior.

QUESTION 31

How Should We Respond To The Death Of A Loved One Who Is A Believer?

Death is the final outcome for human beings living in a sinful world. Once a person dies, there is no hope of doing anything else in this life. All relationships in this world are over. Believers, as well as unbelievers die. We all die.

What is the proper attitude to take when a loved one, who believes in Jesus Christ, dies? Does the Bible provide any guidance on how to respond?

WHAT TO DO WHEN BELIEVERS DIE

When loved ones, who are believers die, our attitude should be one of sadness mixed with joy. The sadness is mainly for ourselves. It certainly should not be for the believer who died. That person is in a better place. Indeed, the loss is ours. Scripture says the following about the death of believer and the proper response.

1. WE MUST REALIZE THAT DEATH IS AN ENEMY

Death is not a friend. In fact, the Bible says that death is a real enemy. Paul wrote the following to the Corinthians.

> The last enemy *that* shall be destroyed *is* death (1 Corinthians 15:26 KJV).

Death robs us. Indeed, the deceased loved one will no longer be part of our lives. On this earth, we will no longer see that person or talk to that person. It is a genuine loss, a heartfelt loss. We should not pretend that it is not. Losing someone we know and love hurts.

2. MOURNING ABOUT DEATH IS APPROPRIATE

We also find that mourning the dead is appropriate. Scripture gives us examples of godly people who mourned at the death of other godly people whom they loved.

DAVID MOURNED THE DEATH OF JONATHAN

We find David mourning for his good friend Jonathan when he died. We read.

> Then David and all the men with him took hold of their clothes and tore them. They mourned and wept and fasted till evening for Saul and his son Jonathan, and for the army of the LORD and for the nation of Israel, because they had fallen by the sword (2 Samuel 1:11-12 NIV).

David went through the normal grieving process. He did not pretend that his good friend Jonathan's death was painless for him. It hurt him deeply.

GODLY BELIEVERS MOURNED STEPHEN'S LOSS

Christians, like everyone else, are not immune to pain when people die. It is not wrong for Christians to mourn. The Bible tells us what took place after the martyr Stephen died.

> Devout men buried Stephen as they mourned loudly for him (Acts 8:2 God's Word).

There was great sorrow at his loss. No longer would they ever have the fellowship of Stephen in this life.

Furthermore, we are told that these men were "devout" or "godly." This informs us that it is proper for godly people to grieve at the death of a fellow believer; especially one they deeply care about.

JESUS MOURNED AT THE DEATH OF LAZARUS

Jesus Himself mourned at the tomb of His dead friend Lazarus. The Bible says that Jesus cried. John wrote.

> Jesus wept (John 11:35 KJV).

Even Jesus could weep at death. If He was allowed to cry, then we certainly are also.

3. THE STING OF DEATH IS GONE FOR THE BELIEVER

Fortunately, Jesus Christ has taken the sting out of death. Paul wrote the following victorious statement to the Corinthians.

> So when this corruptible has put on incorruption, and this mortal has put on immortality, then shall be brought to pass the saying that is written: 'Death is swallowed up in victory." O Death, where *is* your sting? O Hades, where *is* your victory? (1 Corinthians 15:54,55 NKJV).

Death is still our enemy but this enemy will one day be destroyed. Ultimately, death is not victorious over the believer. While it is an enemy, it is a conquered enemy!

4. THERE IS HOPE FOR THE DEAD IN JESUS CHRIST

In Christ Jesus, there is hope for the living and the dead. Paul wrote to the Thessalonians about the genuine hope which each of us has.

> But we do not want you to be uninformed, brothers and sisters, about those who have died, so that you may not grieve as others do who have no hope (1 Thessalonians 4:13 NRSV).

Notice that he did not want the people to be uninformed about this truth. He made it clear that it is proper to be sorrowful when a believer dies, but it is not the same sorrowful feeling as those who have no hope. Christians do mourn when another Christian dies, especially a loved one. However our sorrow is mixed with the hope of something better for the one who passed away.

The Lord Himself is our hope. The psalmist wrote.

> The LORD is close to the brokenhearted and saves those who are crushed in spirit (Psalm 34:18 NIV).

Fortunately, we have hope in Jesus Christ.

5. THERE IS COMFORT FOR THE HURTING

One of the great truths in Scripture is that the comfort we receive from the Lord can also be used to comfort others. Indeed, those who have received comfort can provide comfort for the hurting. Paul wrote the following to the Corinthians about how we help one another.

> Praise the God and Father of our Lord Jesus Christ! He is the Father who is compassionate and the God who gives comfort. He comforts us whenever we suffer. That is why whenever other people suffer, we are able to comfort them by using the same comfort we have received from God (2 Corinthians 1:3-4 God's Word).

This is good news! God allows us to comfort others with the same comfort we received when we had experienced a similar heartbreak. Even in the midst of pain and sorrow, there is comfort which can be given.

6. WE CAN GRIEVE WHEN WE REALIZE WE WILL NEVER SEE A PERSON AGAIN IN THIS LIFE

Not only should Christians grieve for dead loved ones, we may also grieve when we realize that we will not ever see certain loved ones again. As far as this life is concerned, we will never have the pleasure of their company.

This can be illustrated with an experience of the Apostle Paul. He spent much time with the believers in the city of Ephesus. There came a time when he said goodbye to them for the last time. He knew that they would never see him again. He said to them.

> And now I know that none of you, among whom I have gone about proclaiming the kingdom, will ever see my face again (Acts 20:25 NRSV).

After he made a farewell speech, the people were grieved because they would never see him again. We read of their emotional response.

> Everyone cried and hugged and kissed him. They were especially sad because Paul had told them, "You will never see me again" (Acts 20:37,38 CEV).

This type of emotional response is certainly allowable for believers. Therefore it is permitted for us to grieve when we realize we will not see someone again.

PAUL GRIEVED AT THE POSSIBILITY OF THE DEATH OF EPAPHRODITUS

We find Paul grieving at the idea of the possible death of Epaphroditus, a fellow minister. He wrote the following to the Philippians about this grief.

> Still, I think it necessary to send to you Epaphroditus--my brother and co-worker and fellow soldier, your messenger and minister to my need; for he has been longing for all of you, and has been distressed because you heard that he was ill. He was indeed so ill that he nearly died. But God had mercy on him, and not only on him but on me also, so that I would not have one sorrow after another (Philippians 2:25-27 NRSV).

It was proper to him to grieve at the possibility of losing his close friend and fellow-worker. In fact, Paul emphasized that the loss of this man would have caused him tremendous sorrow. Consequently, we can, and should, also grieve at the possibility that someone may soon die and that we may have seen them for the very last time.

THERE ARE MANY REASONS TO GRIEVE

In sum, we can say that the Bible understands what we go through when a fellow believer dies, especially a loved one. However, because we know that this person is with the Lord the feelings we have are bittersweet.

It is also permissible to grieve for someone we love who is about to die whom we may never see again.

Thus, grieving is normal in a number of different circumstances. However, as mentioned, for our loved ones who have put their faith in Jesus Christ our grief is tempered with genuine hope. Indeed, we will see them again! Praise God!

SUMMARY TO QUESTION 31
HOW SHOULD WE RESPOND TO THE DEATH OF A LOVED ONE WHO IS A BELIEVER?

Death is an enemy for all of us. There is no getting around this. When a loved one dies, we should express our grief at their loss. There is nothing wrong with mourning for the dead. Yet the death of Christians is bittersweet. We know they are better off, but we ourselves have suffered loss. The mourning, therefore, is for those of us who are left behind and for our loss of never seeing them again this side of heaven.

We find that mourning is a biblical practice. Scripture gives us examples of believers mourning at the death of others. This includes King David who mourned the death of Jonathan. He was deeply hurt when his best friend died. Scripture records David's words which he wrote about his great loss.

The godly believers who buried the martyr Stephen mourned at his murder. They had suffered a great loss at the death of their beloved friend. Although they knew Stephen was with Jesus, this was still a loss for them. Jesus Himself cried at the tomb of His friend Lazarus. If Jesus can cry at death then so can we. He knows that death brings pain.

Consequently, mourning at the death of another believer, especially a loved one, is not sinful. We should not ever assume that our tears somehow show a lack of faith. They do not. While it is proper to mourn, Christians mourn as those who have genuine hope. Jesus Christ has conquered death. Those who believe in Him will also conquer the grave. The bodies of the dead in Christ will one day be raised.

Because of what Jesus accomplished on the cross, we can be comforted with the thought that we will again see those loved ones who have died in Christ. Therefore, our mourning should be tempered with our understanding that the believer who has died is now in glory.

There is something else which should also be considered. Not only are we allowed to grieve for our dead loved ones, we may also grieve when we realize that we will not see a loved one again. This is what happened in the case of the Apostle Paul and the church at Ephesus. He and the entire leadership were in tears at the thought of never seeing each other again. Thus, it is proper to grieve at the prospect of never again seeing someone who is still alive.

In addition, we find Paul grieving over the possible death of his friend Epaphroditus. Though Epaphroditus did not die, Paul was concerned with the possibility that his beloved fellow-worker in Christ would experience death. This type of grief is also acceptable.

Again, grief is something the Scripture understands and allows. Grief is certainly understandable for the believer who realizes they will never see a loved one again in this life. However, with this grief there is always hope. We will see them again someday!

QUESTION 32

How Should We Respond To The Death Of A Loved One Who May Not Be A Believer?

The death of a loved one is always a loss. However, the death of a loved one, who may have died as an unbeliever, is a cause for even greater sadness. We have sadness that we will not see that loved one again, as well as sadness that they may not have been a believer in Jesus Christ as their Savior. How then should we react to the death of a loved one who may have not believed in Jesus? What should we do?

THEIR FINAL DESTINATION IS IN THE HANDS OF GOD

To begin with, God and God alone will be the Judge of our loved one. Only He knows whether or not they have believed in Christ. While we cannot be comforted with the knowledge that they were a genuine believer, we do not know what may have happened between them and the Lord in their dying moments. In these cases, we leave it in the hands of the Lord.

OUR HEARTS SHOULD DESIRE TO REACH THE LOST

Realizing this should all the more encourage Christians to bring the message of salvation for those who still have a chance, those who are still living. We should desire to be an instrument of the Lord through prayer and our testimony. We are not able to do anything for the dead but we certainly can reach the living.

For example, Paul's feeling toward Israel illustrates the proper attitude toward the lost. He wrote the following to the Book of Romans.

> I am a follower of Christ, and the Holy Spirit is a witness to my conscience. So I tell the truth and I am not lying when I say my heart is broken and I am in great sorrow. I would gladly be placed under God's curse and be separated from Christ for the good of my own people (Romans 9:1-3 CEV).

He had tremendous agony for the lost. He wanted them to know the same Christ that He knew. If it were possible, he would wish himself accursed for their sake. While it was not possible, this shows the depth of his feelings.

THERE IS NO HOPE WITHOUT JESUS CHRIST

The Bible is clear that those who have died without Jesus Christ are without any hope whatsoever. There are no words of comfort that we can give. They have no second chance, no hope of repentance. Only judgment waits. The writer to the Hebrews said.

> And just as people are appointed to die once, and then to face judgment (Hebrews 9:27 NET).

We only live once. After this life judgment awaits all of us. For the believer it consists of rewards for our faithful service. Indeed, judgment day is "reward day."

However, for the nonbeliever there is only condemnation. Therefore, death ends any chance of that person coming to God and obtaining eternal life.

Consequently, it is essential that we reach people who are still alive with the message of Jesus Christ. He is their only hope.

ULTIMATELY, WE DO NOT KNOW THEIR DESTINY

There is something else we must appreciate. The Bible makes it clear that the Lord, and only the Lord, is the Judge of the human race. Judgment is His right alone.

Indeed, only the Lord knows their hearts. The Bible says.

> For he has set a day for judging the world with justice by the man he has appointed, and he proved to everyone who this is by raising him from the dead (Acts 17:31 NLT)

Note that the Bible says that the Lord will judge everyone "with justice" or "with righteousness." Therefore, we should be careful in what we say or think about the eternal destiny of our loved ones. We cannot assume that responsibility. We leave it in the capable hands of the Lord and rest in His goodness and righteousness.

SUMMARY TO QUESTION 32
HOW SHOULD WE RESPOND TO THE DEATH OF A LOVED ONE WHO MAY NOT BE A BELIEVER?

When a friend or a relative dies, it is a sad moment. We are sad, because we have lost someone close to us. It is all the more sad when we are not certain if that person had placed their faith in Christ.

We know that they will not have a second chance to believe after death. Their fate has been eternally determined in this life and in this life alone. There is nothing we, or anyone else, can do for them. Their destiny is fixed.

Consequently, our thoughts and efforts should be directed at those unsaved people who are living. They are still reachable. We should put our time into reaching them with the message of Jesus Christ. The dead are beyond our reach.

As far as those who have died, ultimately we do not know if a person has made a decision to believe in the Lord. Indeed, it is between them and God. Yet the fact there is doubt about a person's relationship with the Lord is a cause for sadness.

However, we must recognize that it is not our personal responsibility to determine the eternal destiny of anyone. We do not have the ability to make such decisions. This belongs to the God of the Bible and to Him alone.

Since we do not have sufficient knowledge to make a determination about those who have died, we should not assume that we know where they are going. This should come as a relief to us. God will judge them and His judgment will be fair and right. In the end, this is all we really need to know.

How Are We To Understand People Who Have Claimed To Have Visions Of Heaven Or Hell Right Before Their Death? (Deathbed Visions)

There have been a number of people who have claimed to have some type of supernatural or heavenly vision shortly before the time of their death. Among other things, these are known as "deathbed visions."

What are these things? Are they real? How should we respond to the idea that certain people have had these experiences immediately prior to death? What does the Bible say about this?

DEATHBED VISIONS AND NEAR DEATH EXPERIENCES

A deathbed experience is not the same as a "near death experience." In a so-called near death experience the person dies, comes back to life, and then tells us what the other side is like.

A deathbed experience, or a deathbed vision, refers to what people who claim to actually see what the next world consists of. Before they lose their life, they have visions of what they are about to experience in the realm of the dead. Soon thereafter they pass on to the next world.

However, contrary to those who claim to have had near death experiences, these people do *not* come back to tell us if their visions were accurate.

These deathbed visions include seeing deceased loved ones, religious figures such as Moses, Jesus, or heaven itself. There have also been reports of people seeing the darkness of hell with all its horror. Those reports do not get as well-publicized.

A BIBLICAL EXAMPLE OF A DEATHBED VISION: STEPHEN

While there are biblical examples of people who have died and then have come back to life, none of them have said anything about their experience in the realm of the dead; at least nothing that was recorded in the Bible.

However, we do have an example of one who had a deathbed vision; the martyr Stephen. When Stephen, the first martyr of the Christian church was about to be murdered by a hostile crowd, he testified to seeing Jesus waiting for Him. Scripture puts it this way.

> When the council members heard Stephen's speech, they were angry and furious. But Stephen was filled with the Holy Spirit. He looked toward heaven, where he saw our glorious God and Jesus standing at his right side. Then Stephen said, "I see heaven open and the Son of Man standing at the right side of God!" (Acts 7:54-56 CEV).

Stephen was granted a vision of heaven with Jesus Christ welcoming him home. The description of Jesus by Stephen is significant. All other portrayals of the glorified Christ have him sitting at the right hand of God the Father. Here the Lord is standing. Jesus is waiting to welcome one of his saints to heaven. Therefore, the idea of some type of heavenly deathbed vision is consistent with biblical teaching.

Ultimately, of course, we do not know what really happens to those who have had these visions because there is no way to test them.

Yet when a believer in Jesus Christ is about to die, and testifies to seeing heaven opening up to receive them, we should not doubt what they are saying.

In the same manner, we should not doubt when unbelievers have visions of terror and judgment when they are about die. Their eternity awaits and it too is calling them to where they will soon go.

SUMMARY TO QUESTION 33
HOW ARE WE TO UNDERSTAND PEOPLE WHO HAVE CLAIMED TO HAVE HAD VISIONS OF HEAVEN OR HELL RIGHT BEFORE THEIR DEATH? (DEATHBED VISIONS)

Deathbed visions are certain experiences which people claim they are having as they are about to die. Many people have given testimony to seeing departed loves, the face of Jesus, or some other wonderful sight as they slip into eternity.

Deathbed visions are different from near death experiences. In a near death experience, a person claims to have died and then come back from the realm of the dead. Their experience is of one who has died and then comes back to life. In near death experiences the person relates what the other side is like from one who had been there temporarily.

The deathbed vision consists of visions of a person who is about to die. They do not return from the dead to tell us if their vision was correct. Thus, we have no way of knowing if what they saw was actually there.

While nobody can prove or disprove the validity of their experience, a deathbed vision for the believer is consistent with the teaching of Scripture. We are told that the martyr Stephen, when he was about to be murdered, saw a vision of Jesus Christ standing at the right hand of God the Father. Jesus was waiting to receive Stephen into heaven.

We also note that Jesus was not in His usual position of sitting at the right hand of the Father; He actually stood up to welcome Stephen! What a tremendous comfort it is to believers to know that Jesus is ready to welcome those who have believed in Him. This deathbed vision was given to encourage Stephen as well as those of us who read about it. Believers, who are about to die, are welcomed into the presence of the Lord.

This being the case, we should not doubt the possibility or the actuality of other believers having similar experiences when they are about to die. Consequently, we should not discount such testimonies.

The same can be said for the experiences of unbelievers who are about to die. They too testify to visions of the next world. However, in their case, it is the darkness in which they are about to enter.

These visions of believers and unbelievers are consistent of what we know about the afterlife. Some will enter the presence of Jesus Christ while others will spend a lonely Christless eternity. This is the clear teaching of Scripture.

QUESTION 34

How Are We To Understand Claims Of People Who Say They Have Died, Gone To Heaven Or Hell, And Then Returned? (Near Death Experiences)

Deathbed visions, people getting a glimpse of the eternity they are about to enter, are likely to be actual experiences by those who are about to depart from this world.

However, the same cannot be said for what is known as "near death experiences." This term refers to testimonies of people who have been pronounced dead yet come back to life after a short period of time. Certain people have claimed that during the interval between death and resuscitation they had experiences of the afterlife. Testimonies vary as to what is seen in the next world.

Some people testify to a peaceful experience. Usually, they are assured that there is indeed an afterlife where everything is wonderful for every person. In other words, death does not have to be feared because everyone will be received in some sort of eternal bliss once they have died.

As can be imagined, this sort of testimony is well-received by the public which fears death and does not want to think about it.

What should we make of such testimonies of a blissful afterlife? Should we believe these people really got a glimpse of the next world?

1. THE ONLY RELIABLE SOURCE IS SCRIPTURE

To begin with, the only authoritative source on the next life is what is found in God's Word, the Bible. Scripture, and Scripture alone, has the final say on all matters.

Thus, whatever anyone says about any topic, which the Bible touches upon, must conform to Scripture. If not, we simply do not believe it.

How then do testimonies of near death experiences compare to what the Bible says? Should we believe them? There are a number of points we need to make.

2. THERE ARE ACCOUNTS OF PEOPLE WHO HAVE COME BACK TO LIFE

There are accounts of biblical characters which were brought back from the dead, or resuscitated. We find them recorded in both testaments.

A. OLD TESTAMENT EXAMPLES

There are three examples in the Old Testament of people coming back to life. They can be listed as follows.

ELIJAH RAISED A CHILD FROM THE DEAD (1 KINGS 17:20-22)

Scripture testifies of the prophet Elijah bringing a child back from the dead. However, there is no record of the child speaking. The only thing mentioned is that the child returned to life. Nothing more.

ELISHA BROUGHT A CHILD BACK TO LIFE (2 KINGS 4:32-37)

Elisha the prophet performed a similar miracle of bringing a child back to life. As was true in the case of Elijah, no words of the child are recorded.

THE BONES OF ELISHA BROUGHT A MAN BACK TO LIFE (2 KINGS 13:20-21)

There is also an instance of the dead body of Elisha bringing a dead man back to life. We read what took place in Second Kings.

Elisha died and was buried. Moabite raiding parties invaded the land at the beginning of the year. One day some men were burying a man when they spotted a raiding party. So they threw the dead man into Elisha's tomb. When the body touched Elisha's bones, the dead man came to life and stood on his feet (2 Kings 13:20-21 NET)

Again, nothing is recorded about what the man may have said after he was resuscitated.

In none of these examples, do we find any testimony of what life in the unseen realm consisted of. No word is given as to what they experienced.

B. NEW TESTAMENT EXAMPLES

In the New Testament we have a number of stories of people being brought back from the dead. They are as follows.

JAIRUS DAUGHTER (LUKE 8:49-55)

Jesus brought back to life the daughter of a man named Jairus. She had just recently died when Jesus made her live again. However, there is no record of her saying anything after she was resuscitated.

THE WIDOW OF NAIN'S SON (LUKE 7:11-15)

Luke records Jesus resuscitating the son of a widow from the city of Nain. She was on her way to bury her son when Jesus brought him back from the dead. Scripture does not record him speaking.

LAZARUS (JOHN 11)

Lazarus was dead four days when Jesus brought him back to life. Although the Bible says that Lazarus held a feast for Jesus after his resuscitation, no recorded words of Lazarus are found in the New Testament.

DORCAS (ACTS 9:36-41)

Dorcas, or Tabitha, was a woman who was a great asset to the early church. When she died the believers asked Peter if he would bring her back to life. The Lord gave him the ability to do so. However, there was nothing written in Scripture about anything she may have said about her death experience.

EUTYCHUS (ACTS 20:7-12)

Eutychus was a young man who fell to his death after having fallen asleep listening to a message from the Apostle Paul. Like the other biblical characters, nothing is recorded of his experience in the realm of the dead.

Each of these people had died and were brought back to life. Yet absolutely nothing is recorded in Scripture as to what they saw or what they experienced. We do not know if they told anyone about what happened to them during the time they were dead. Nothing has been recorded.

3. THERE IS NO BIBLICAL COMMAND TO DISCOVER TRUTH FROM THOSE WHO HAVE DIED

Not only do we find the Scriptures silent as to what happened to those who had died and were brought back to life, the Bible does not command us to discover anything about the afterlife from those who have had such an experience. They are not the people who should be giving us information about what the world of the dead is like.

4. THE APOSTLE PAUL DID NOT DESCRIBE HIS EXPERIENCE IN THE WORLD OF THE DEAD

We only have one biblical testimony of an individual who went to the realm of the dead and then came back to tell us about it, the Apostle Paul. He had an experience where he was caught up to the presence of the Lord. Interestingly, he did not reveal anything which happened to him while he was there. He gave the following testimony to the church in Corinth.

> I have to brag. There is nothing to be gained by it, but I must brag about the visions and other things that the Lord has shown me. I know about one of Christ's followers who was taken up into the third heaven fourteen years ago. I don't know if the man was still in his body when it happened, but God certainly knows. As I said, only God really knows if this man was in his body at the time. But he was taken up into paradise, where he heard things that are too wonderful to tell (2 Corinthians 12:1-4 CEV).

Note well what he said. Paul testified that he was not able to give any specifics about the afterlife. He could only testify that words could not express the wonderful situation in which believers would find themselves.

Furthermore, there were things about this experience which he himself was not certain of. Paul said that he did not know whether he was still in his body or out of his body. If the Apostle Paul could not testify with any certainty about his near death experience, then we should not listen to anyone else who attempts to give a similar testimony of their experience. They have no credibility whatsoever.

There is one other thing we must observe. This experience of Paul was only mentioned this one time in his writings. Indeed, we never find him sharing this experience again! Indeed, Paul never pointed to it to prove that the afterlife existed. Never.

What do we find from his writings that give proof that there is an afterlife? It was the resurrection of Jesus Christ from the dead which demonstrates that an afterlife exists. He wrote.

> And if Christ has not been raised, then your faith is useless and you are still guilty of your sins. In that case, all who have

died believing in Christ are lost! . . . But in fact, Christ has been raised from the dead. He is the first of a great harvest of all who have died (1 Corinthians 15:17-18,20 NLT).

Therefore, we should follow the example of Paul. Indeed, our job is to proclaim what the Scriptures have to say about proof of the afterlife rather than looking to the testimonies of people who claim to have had these near death experiences. This is the proper perspective for believers.

5. JOHN HAD VISIONS OF HEAVEN BUT DID NOT HAVE A NEAR DEATH EXPERIENCE

The only New Testament writer who tells us anything about conditions in heaven is the Apostle John. In the Book of Revelation, we have a number of things told to us by him. However, he merely had visions of heaven and was permitted to give some of the details. Yet this was not a testimony of one who had died and visited the realm of the dead. Indeed, it was the testimony of a person who was given visions of the afterlife while he was still alive.

6. WE CANNOT TRUST THE TESTIMONIES OF THOSE WHO HAD NEAR DEATH EXPERIENCES

From the biblical evidence we conclude that we cannot trust the testimonies of those who have claimed to have had near death experiences which reveal that everything is great for everyone in the afterlife. No matter what their motives may be, or how sincere they believe what they experienced was real, their testimony must be rejected. There are a number of reasons as to why this is so.

DEATH IS NOT WONDERFUL FOR EVERYONE

For one thing, the Bible teaches that the afterlife will not be wonderful for everyone. Indeed, there are only two destinies which are possible for each individual. One destiny is for believers. They will spend eternity with God. In eternity, these believers will live in unimaginable wonder. This is the teaching of Scripture.

Scripture, however, teaches another destiny for those who have rejected God's truth. This is known as hell, or the lake of fire. Eternity for these people will be horrible beyond words.

GOD'S WRATH RESTS UPON UNBELIEVERS

In fact, God's wrath or anger continually rests upon them. The Bible describes these two destinations in the following manner.

> The one who believes in the Son has eternal life, but the one who refuses to believe in the Son will not see life; instead, the wrath of God remains on him (John 3:36 HCSB).

Therefore, Scripture speaks of heaven for some but the punishment of hell for others. Those who say that the afterlife is wonderful for everyone are giving people an idea of what is to come which is totally contradictory to the Word of God.

SATAN LIES ABOUT WHAT GOD HAS SAID

What about the many descriptions of a "white light" which those who have had the near death experience speak about? Should this be understood as a sign that they have come into God's presence. The Bible does say that God is light and there is no darkness in Him.

> This is the message we have heard from him and declare to you: God is light; in him there is no darkness at all (1 John 1:5 NIV).

However, we must also remember how Satan, the great adversary of the Lord, is described in Scripture; as an angel of light. The Apostle Paul wrote about false apostles who disguised themselves as true ministers of Christ. He said.

These people are false apostles. They have fooled you by disguising themselves as apostles of Christ. But I am not surprised! Even Satan can disguise himself as an angel of light (2 Corinthians 11:13,14 NLT).

Satan's job is to fool people. Therefore, he would want people to think everything is fantastic in the afterlife for everyone. Yet the Bible says that not everyone will be in God's presence in the next world. Satan would certainly not want people to know about the coming judgment for unbelievers. Consequently, the white light gives unbelievers a false sense of security. Only a relationship with Jesus Christ can give a person true security about the afterlife.

NOT ALL REPORTS OF THE AFTERLIFE ARE POSITIVE

There is one more thing which should be stressed. While many report positive experiences in their near death experiences, there have been people who have experienced sheer horror. Who is correct? Is it the ones which say everything is wonderful or the ones who are terrified with what they supposedly see? Upon what basis do we make the decision?

Unless we have God's Word as our foundation, we do not have any basis to judge these so-called experiences. How do we know the person is not a deceiver, one who was deceived, or someone whose description of the afterlife merely reflects chemicals released in their brain. We simply do not know. Indeed, we cannot know.

THESE PEOPLE DID NOT REMAIN DEAD

Remember something else; these people did not remain dead. They came back to life. So they are not really telling us about what it means to be once-and-for-all dead. Indeed, they are only telling us what they think it means to be lifeless for *a short period of time.* At best, they are telling us what they know, or think they know, about the time of transition from life to death.

However, we want to know about what happens after death, not what may or may not occur in some transitional moment when the person is neither dead nor living. Thus, they are no help to us whatsoever.

Let's stay with the only One which gives us authoritative information about the other side, Jesus Christ. We read the following in the Book of Revelation about why Christians should not fear death.

> When I saw him, I fell at his feet as dead. But he laid his right hand on me and said, "Don't be afraid! I am the First and the Last. I am the living one who died. Look, I am alive forever and ever! And I hold the keys of death and the grave" (Revelation 1:17-18 NLT).

Jesus tells believers not to be afraid. He has been there! He has experienced death and He informs us what it is like on the "other side."

THE TEACHINGS OF THE BIBLE ARE SUFFICIENT!

In sum, the truth about what happens after death comes from the Bible and from it alone. The teachings of Scripture are sufficient; we do not need anything added to it. Indeed, no other source is trustworthy and no other source is necessary!

SUMMARY TO QUESTION 34
HOW ARE WE TO UNDERSTAND CLAIMS OF PEOPLE WHO SAY THEY HAVE DIED, GONE TO HEAVEN OR HELL, AND THEN RETURNED? (NEAR DEATH EXPERIENCES)

There have been people who have testified to their near death experience. While actually being dead, they claimed to have had certain experiences of the next world. Now that they have returned, they want to inform us as to what it is actually like to be dead, as well as what the next world consists of. They believe that they have the answer!

Usually these experiences tout how wonderful it is in the next world and that no one should be fearful of death. Judgment is rarely, if ever, mentioned. These messages lull people into thinking that death is not something to be feared even if they do not believe in any sort of God. Very few people speak of going to hell for this short period of time when they were dead.

These testimonies are found inadequate when compared with Scripture. In fact, there are many reasons why we should not trust them.

First, while there are a number of instances recorded in the Bible where people actually returned from the dead, none of them said anything that was eventually put into writing. If they did describe their experiences we do not know about it.

The Apostle Paul testified that he too spent some time in the unseen realm of the dead. However, he did not give us any details as to what happened to him; only that his experience was too wonderful for words. In fact, he was specifically told that he was not allowed to divulge any details. If Paul could not reveal the details then neither should we expect anyone else to receive specific details of the next world.

In addition, even with this experience, we never again read of Paul referring to it. Never do we find him using what happened to him to prove that there is a life beyond this life. What we do find is Paul emphasizing the resurrection of Jesus Christ from the dead. This is our hope of the afterlife!

Consequently, we should follow his example and proclaim the resurrection of Christ rather than the testimonies of people who have claimed to have had these near death experiences. Following his example should help us keep this issue in the proper perspective.

There is something else. We do have descriptions of the heavenly realm from the writings of the Apostle John in the Book of Revelation. However, John did not die and go to heaven; his words are merely based upon visions he received.

Therefore, we cannot, and should not, trust the testimonies of those who say they have gone to the next world and have returned. Whatever they said they had seen, or thought they had seen, has to be evaluated in light of God's Word.

Those who testify that everything is wonderful in the next life for everyone are denying one of the basic truths of Scripture. Everything will not be wonderful for every person.

Scripture says all humans have a spirit or soul. This is the real "us." This spirit or soul of ours will exist forever. However, we will not all live in the same wonderful place. For those who have rejected God's truth, only punishment awaits them. This punishment is spoken of in the most dreadful of terms.

There is something else we must remember; not all of the near death testimonies are positive. There are those who relate that sheer terror greeted them in the next world. This is more in keeping in line with what the Bible says about the fate of the unbelievers. They will suffer God's wrath while believers, and believers alone, will experience all the wonders of the heavenly realm.

One final thing which should be emphasized concerns the nature of this experience. These people did not really die. The fact that they came back to life proves the point. At best, they were in-between life and death for a short period of time.

Consequently, whatever they tell us is not about what it means to be dead and to remain dead. Nobody can answer that question except God Himself. Jesus Christ, God the Son, died and remained dead for three days before He was raised from the dead. He, and He alone, can tell us what it is like on the other side. Those who have had near death experiences are only lifeless for the shortest of times. Thus, their testimony is meaningless.

All things considered, we should not give any serious attention to those who have claimed to have had near death experiences; they cannot teach us anything about the afterlife. The only authoritative source which we have is the Bible, the Word of the living God. No other source is needed. Indeed, the Bible, and the Bible alone, is our all-sufficient guide to this life and to the next.

QUESTION 35

In The Light Of Eternity, How Should We Live A Life That Is Pleasing To God?

We now come to our last question. Once we understand what the Bible has to say about the subjects of death, dying and the afterlife, we should then go about living our lives in light of these truths. Thus, we want to know how we can live a life pleasing to God in the light of the eternity that awaits us. The Bible makes certain facts clear with respect to our life.

1. WE MUST REALIZE THAT LIFE IS SHORT

First, life here upon earth is only for a relatively short time. We find statements in the Old Testament that speak of the shortness of life. We read in Job.

> Man born of woman is of few days and full of trouble. He springs up like a flower and withers away; like a fleeting shadow, he does not endure (Job 14:1-2 NIV).

The Bible confirms the fact that life is short.

LIFE IS COMPARED TO A BREATH

Our life here upon earth is compared to a breath. It comes and goes so very quickly. The psalmist wrote.

You have made my days a mere handbreadth; the span of my years is as nothing before you. Each man's life is but a breath (Psalm 39:5 NIV).

LIFE VANISHES LIKE SMOKE

In another place, the psalmist compared our life here on earth to smoke which quickly vanishes. He wrote.

For my days vanish like smoke; my bones burn like glowing embers (Psalm 102:3 NIV).

LIFE IS COMPARED TO DREAMS THAT DISAPPEAR AND GRASS WHICH WITHERS

In a further reference, the psalmist wrote about the Lord sweeping away people like dreams that disappear and grass that withers. He wrote.

You sweep people away like dreams that disappear or like grass that springs up in the morning. In the morning it blooms and flourishes, but by evening it is dry and withered (Psalm 90:5-6 NLT).

Dreams come and go in an instant. Grass grows then withers. So goes our life.

LIFE IS LIKE A MIST

The New Testament also emphasizes that life is short. James compares it to mist or fog. He wrote the following.

Yet you do not even know what tomorrow will bring. What is your life? For you are a mist that appears for a little while and then vanishes (James 4:14 NRSV).

As the mist appears for a short time, our lives come and go quickly.

All of these biblical analogies make it clear that life is short.

2. WE MUST UNDERSTAND THAT DEATH COMES UNEXPECTED

Not only is life short, death comes to human beings unexpectedly. It can come at any time. None of us is guaranteed we will live out this very day.

We know we are going to die, but we do not know when we will die, where we will die, or how we will die. We read in Proverbs.

> Don't brag about tomorrow! Each day brings its own surprises (Proverbs 27:1 CEV).

Indeed, none of us knows what today will bring.

The day of our death is unknown to us. When the patriarch Isaac grew old, he said.

> I am now an old man and don't know the day of my death (Genesis 27:2 NIV).

None of us know that day.

Indeed, death often comes without any warning. In Ecclesiastes we read.

> No one knows when his time will come. Like fish that are caught in a cruel net or birds caught in a snare, humans are trapped by a disaster when it suddenly strikes them (Ecclesiastes 9:12 God's Word).

Usually we have no warning that death is coming.

3. WE NEED TO MAKE THE MOST OF THE TIME

Since life is short, and we do not know when we will die, we need to make the most of the time that we do have. Consequently, all of us should live each day in light of eternity. Paul told believers.

Make the most of every opportunity for doing good in these
evil days (Ephesians 5:16 NLT).

Since each day may be our last, this should cause us to make the most
of the time that we have. We are not promised that we will be around
tomorrow.

Paul wrote to the Romans about what we should be doing as we make
the most of the time that we do have.

> Don't be lazy in showing your devotion. Use your energy
> to serve the Lord. Be happy in your confidence, be patient
> in trouble, and pray continually. Share what you have
> with God's people who are in need. Be hospitable. Bless
> those who persecute you. Bless them, and don't curse them
> (Romans 12:11-14 God's Word).

Since the time is short we need to make the most of every single day.
We should never waste any time but rather use our energy to serve the
Lord.

WE ARE TO SHINE LIKE THE STARS

Indeed, we are to shine like the stars in the sky. We read in Philippians.

> Do everything without grumbling and arguing, so that you
> may be blameless and pure, children of God who are faultless
> in a crooked and perverted generation, among whom you
> shine like stars in the world (Philippians 2:14-15 HCSB).

Believers are to be "the light of the world" bringing them the message
of Christ.

WE SHOULD STORE UP TREASURE IN HEAVEN

In addition, Jesus said that we are to lay up treasure in heaven. In the
Sermon on the Mount, Matthew records Him saying the following.

Do not lay up for yourselves treasures on earth, where moth and rust destroy and where thieves break in and steal; but lay up for yourselves treasures in heaven, where neither moth nor rust destroys and where thieves do not break in and steal (Matthew 6:19,20 NKJV).

Our treasures should be stored where no one can rob them. This is in God's home in heaven. Nobody can steal them if they are with Him.

WE SHOULD BE MOTIVATED TO TELL OTHERS ABOUT JESUS

We should also be motivated to tell others about Jesus as we live in the light of eternity. Indeed, it is God's desire that all would come to know Him. Peter wrote.

The Lord is not slow about his promise, as some think of slowness, but is patient with you, not wanting any to perish, but all to come to repentance (2 Peter 3:9 NRSV).

There is a reason for the delay of God's judgment. He wants more people to believe in Him. His patience is reflected in this desire for these lost souls to turn to Him in faith. Our responsibility is to get the Word of God out to them so they can believe in Christ.

The Bible says that believers bring the fragrance of life to those who are perishing. Paul wrote to the Corinthians.

For we are the aroma of Christ to God among those who are being saved and among those who are perishing (2 Corinthians 2:15 NRSV).

Our desire should be to tell others the good news about Jesus.

4. WE SHOULD HAVE NO ULTIMATE FEAR OF DEATH

As we have previously noted, it is not wrong to have a natural fear of death. We have never experienced what it means to be dead, and eternity is certainly a long time! This of course, can lead us to be concerned about our own death.

Though there is the natural human fear that each of us have about death, there is also the confidence which we can have that we will be with the Lord. Ultimately, there is nothing to fear in death because it is a transition into something much better. We must always remember this.

5. WE SHOULD REALIZE THAT OUR DECISIONS HAVE ETERNAL CONSEQUENCES

Consequently, the decisions we make in this life determine where we will spend the next. We should, therefore, make certain that the right decisions are made. The final states are fixed. Indeed, there is no second chance after we are gone.

6. HEAVEN SHOULD BE ON OUR MIND

Finally, we should have heaven constantly on our mind so as to have an impact in this world. C.S. Lewis said it well.

It is since Christians have largely ceased to think of the other world that they have become so ineffective in this. Aim at heaven and you will get earth thrown in; aim at earth and you will get neither.

Realizing that life is short should cause us to make the most of each day. Eternity is not far off for any of us. The key question that each of us has to answer is this, "Am I ready to meet my Maker?"

SUMMARY TO QUESTION 35
IN THE LIGHT OF ETERNITY, HOW SHOULD WE LIVE A LIFE THAT IS PLEASING TO GOD?

Eternity is ahead for each of us. The Bible tells us how to live in light of eternity. There are a number of things we should be doing.

First, we must first realize that life is short. In the Old Testament it is compared to a breath. The New Testament compares it to the mist that comes and goes. We are not here on earth for very long. Hence, we need to make the most of the time.

Furthermore, death usually comes without warning. Most of us will have no idea when we are going to die, how we are going to die, or where we are going to die. But we do know that we will indeed die. We need to be ready.

Since death usually comes unexpectedly we all need to make the most of the time that we have. Our view of eternity will affect the way in which we live today. Time should be spent living a godly life.

One of the things we should concentrate upon is telling others the "good news" about Jesus. This is the reason that we are still here. We need to make Him known to the lost so that they too can have the gift of salvation and genuine hope for the future.

Indeed, the message of Jesus is a message of hope. It is our responsibility to share that message.

To sum up, living a life that is pleasing to the Lord should be our main goal. Only then will we achieve true happiness and fulfillment.

Finally, though we live here upon the earth, heaven should constantly be on our mind. We should always be ready to meet our Maker. Who knows when this will be? Perhaps it will be today.

OUR NEXT BOOK IN THE
AFTERLIFE SERIES: VOLUME 2
What Happens
One Second After We Die?

Now that we have looked at what the Scripture has to say about how we are to conduct our lives in light of eternity, we will next examine what the Bible has to say about the state of people immediately after they die – the intermediate or the in-between state. We will explore questions such as the following.

What Happens To A Believer Immediately Upon Death?

Do The Dead Have A Body In Their Intermediate State?

Should The Living Pray For The Dead?

Is There Such A Place As Purgatory?

Are People Conscious After Death Or Are They Asleep?

This next book in our series will clarify what the Bible says, and what it does not say, regarding the state of those who have died.

About the Author

Don Stewart is a graduate of Biola University and Talbot Theological Seminary (with the highest honors).

Don is a best-selling and award-winning author having authored, or co-authored, over seventy books. This includes the best-selling *Answers to Tough Questions*, with Josh McDowell, as well as the award-winning book *Family Handbook of Christian Knowledge: The Bible*. His various writings have been translated into over thirty different languages and have sold over a million copies.

Don has traveled around the world proclaiming and defending the historic Christian faith. He has also taught both Hebrew and Greek at the undergraduate level and Greek at the graduate level.

76835835R00153

Made in the USA
San Bernardino, CA
16 May 2018